THE WOUNDED
BODY OF CHRIST

Mel Stombel
" 85 "

EARL PAULK

DEDICATION:

To the Church universal and the members and staff of Chapel Hill Harvester Church who have devoted themselves to bringing healing to "The Wounded Body of Christ."

TABLE OF CONTENTS

EARL P. PAULK

Bishop Earl P. Paulk is Senior Pastor of Chapel Hill Harvester Church located in Decatur, Georgia. Chapel Hill Harvester Church has eighteen full-time pastors serving a local parish of over four thousand people with thousands more receiving ministry by television and radio in the Atlanta and North Georgia areas. Both the **Harvester Hour** and the **K-Dimension** program are broadcast weekly on the P.T.L. Satellite Network as well as on other television channels throughout the nation.

Pastor Paulk holds a Bachelor of Arts Degree from Furman University which is a Baptist institution, and a Master of Divinity Degree from the Candler School of Theology, Emory University, which is a Methodist seminary. As the son of a world leader in the classical Pentecostal Church, Doctor Earl P. Paulk Sr., a former Assistant GeneralOverseer of the Church of God, Pastor Paulk has an ecumenical understanding enjoyed by few church leaders in the world today.

Chapel Hill Harvester Church, under the guidance and direction of Earl Paulk, has become a successful working prototype of a true Kingdom church, with foundations rooted and grounded in the Kingdom principles. Among the many outreaches of the Body of Christ at Chapel Hill is ALPHA, a six-year-old youth ministry which draws 800-1200 teenagers every Monday night to worship, praise and to hear anointed preaching and teaching. The church ministries include a home for unwed mothers; a licensed child placement agency; a weekly outreach to the chemically addicted and their families; a special ministry to homosexuals; plus outreach programs to nursing homes, prisons, and spiritually and economically depressed communities.

Chapel Hill Harvester Church is the tangible expression of God's love through the visionary efforts of Bishop Earl Paulk, his wife, Norma, and founding Pastors Don and Clariece Paulk.

FOREWORD

Under normal circumstances a notable personality might be asked to provide some insight into the contents of this book or to make laudatory remarks about its author. In doing so, sales might be increased by bringing the popularity of that person to be associated with the book. However the message of this book speaks for itself - no further credibility need be established than that of the Holy Spirit. The truth contained herein is inspired by God Himself to bring a soothing balm to heal the deepest scars within the Church, the Body of Christ.

No other acknowledgement need be made than the acknowledgement of Him, the author and finisher of our faith - and the guiding force behind this vital message.

The sincerest prayer of the author, and of those associated with this book, is that all who read these words will do so with anointed eyes and hearts. May this message be one that reaches from deep to deep - and Spirit to spirit.

SELAH

INTRODUCTION

Where is the Balm of Gilead within the Church of Jesus Christ today? Divisions among Christians have never been more pronounced or more widespread. Prejudices have divided the Body of Christ in an age when a dying, unsaved world rejects the message of the gospel of the Kingdom on the basis of the disunity and competition they see among Christians.

Deep wounds in the Body of Christ require the Balm of Gilead to restore and to heal the Body until it becomes that glorified Church which is the Bride of Jesus Christ.

WHAT ARE THE WOUNDS?

Disagreements over matters of liturgy and forms of worship divide Christians and focus their attention on the order of worship and format of prayers rather than on the One who is worshipped and who hears the prayers of believers.

Throughout the Body of Christ, attitudes of judgment and exclusivism separate Christians in churches within a community. The "We have no need of them" attitude is a wound in the Body of Christ.

Racial divisions continue to exclude and to divide many believers in neighborhoods and schools as well as churches where Jesus' words are reverently quoted, "Whosoever will, come unto me."

Divorced Christians are allowed no opportunity to minister regardless of the circumstances of their divorces, their gifts from God, or their desire to serve the Lord after He has provided spiritual restoration to their lives.

Women are told by many churches that they may minister only in very restricted areas of service. These limitations hinder the flow of the Holy Spirit in places where women are never allowed to publicly minister to the Body their spiritual gifts from God.

Christians continue to focus on differences of doctrine and methods instead of opening their hearts to the spirit of Jesus' prayer, "Father, make them one."

WHAT IS THE RESULT?

Until the Balm of Gilead is applied to the Body of Christ, the Church will never realize the voice of authority which will make Christ's enemies His footstool (Acts 2:35). The wounds in the Body of Christ result in divisions and strife and alienation among believers. Christians are left without a vision, a cause, or a purpose in their lives.

Wounds in the Body of Christ make the Church's ministry and solutions to the problems in our world diffused and ineffective. Within the Church, families continue to fall apart and youth searching for answers to their questions look elsewhere. The visible wounds in the Body of Christ prevent the Church from moving in power to break the bondages in people's lives. The Church appears ineffective in offering alternatives to such prisons as homosexuality, unwed pregnancies, abortion, alcoholism and drug addictions.

An unsaved world looks to the Church in hopeless desperation, and all it can see are internal wounds, strife and wars.

WHAT IS THE BALM OF GILEAD?

The Balm of Gilead is the spiritual salve to heal the wounds in the Body of Christ. The Balm of Gilead is both a powerful medicine to fight disease and an effective healing salve of restoration. I believe that the Balm of Gilead is applied to the Body of Christ in three inseparable steps.

First, the Balm of Gilead is applied at the TABLE OF THE LORD. Christians are admonished to judge themselves before coming to the Lord's table. The table of the Lord is a place of unity for those willing to follow Jesus, and the table is a place of division for those who choose to go their own way. Individual discernment is essential before a believer can unite his spirit with the Spirit of Jesus Christ in His Body.

> *But let each man examine himself and so let him eat of that bread and drink of that cup. For he that eateth and drinketh unworthily, eateth and drinketh damnation to himself, not discerning the Lord's body. For this cause many are weak and sickly among you, and many sleep. For if we judge ourselves, we should not be judged. But when we are judged, we are chastened by the Lord, that we should not be condemned with the world. (I Corinthians 11:28-32)*

Secondly, the Balm of Gilead is applied when we FOCUS OUR HEARTS ON JESUS. His thoughts, concerns and love become ours. His eyes and ears and voice and arms touch the world through us. We move in boldness, power and authority. "Herein is our love made perfect, that we may have boldness in the day of judgment: because as He is, so also are we in this world" (I John 4:17).

And finally, the Balm of Gilead is applied when we FORGIVE AND RESTORE EACH OTHER. Wounds in the Body of Christ are healed when the Church becomes a City of Refuge. Christians begin covering the weaknesses and failures of their brothers and sisters in love. Believers begin to mature by trusting the Jesus in one another. We begin to move toward each other in compassion, fellowship and unity of faith.

> *Till we all come in the unity of the faith, and of the knowledge of the Son of God, unto a perfect man, unto the measure of the fullness of Christ. That we henceforth be no more children, tossed to and fro, and carried about with every wind of doctrine, by the sleight of men, and cunning craftiness whereby they lie in wait to deceive; But speaking the truth in love, may grow up into him, in all things, which is the head, even Christ. (Ephesians 4:13-15)*

The Balm of Gilead heals the Church so that she is made ready to be the Bride of Christ. Only in full maturity will she be able to rule and reign forever with Him. And when the healing of the Body of Christ is finally accomplished, the Spirit and the Bride say, "Even so, Come Lord Jesus!"

CHAPTER ONE
THE WOUNDED BODY OF JESUS

Holy men of old were moved upon by the Holy Spirit and the revelation given them is God's Word in the Holy Scriptures. Is God speaking any less today through holy men called of God to bring a message through revelation to this generation? The writer of Hebrews reminds us that in times past, God spoke to the fathers by the prophets but "...hath in these last days spoken unto us by his Son, whom he hath appointed heir of all things..." (Hebrews 1:2). It is through this message of Jesus Christ that His Body is being perfected or matured today.

Jesus said of those in His day that they would garnish the tombs of the prophets of old who had been killed by their parents, but would not hear the God-given revelation through the prophets of their day (Matthew 23:29-31). How much this is like unto our day. We wave our Bibles and cry, "This is the Word of God." Indeed it is God's Word, but the Holy Spirit yet brings revelation to this generation today that is no less God's Word. Paul said of the church at Thessalonica that they had received the Word of God which he had spoken unto them, "...not as the word of men, but as it is in truth, the word of God..." (I Thessalonians 2:13).

When the Holy Spirit descended on the day of Pentecost, there came a tremendous prophetic utterance. Peter said, "And it shall come to pass in the last days, saith God, I will pour out my Spirit upon all flesh: and your sons and your daughters shall prophesy, and your young men shall see visions, and your old men shall dream dreams" (Acts 2:17). We have little difficulty with sons and daughters prophesying, but what about

visions and dreams? Is this any less of a promise for the
last days?

In the midst of our humanity, God opens the windows of revelation and begins to speak to us. He said
that in the last days there would be two primary means
by which He would bring His pure Word to us: by
visions and by **dreams.** Both dreams and visions will
contain God's revelation. We cannot go off somewhere
and choose the time when we want to receive a revelation from God. Revelation comes in the midst of our
daily walk as our vision becomes clear and in our times
of sleep as our dreams come to us.

It was in one of those sleeping hours that God spoke
to me in a dream. In that dream, the Holy Spirit took me
back to the place where this ministry began. I was not
taken all the way back to Phoenix, Arizona where the
vision was first given, but back to Euclid Avenue in
Atlanta, Georgia where it began to be literally lived out
in the old St John's Lutheran Church and the First
Christian Missionary Alliance Church, two buildings we
later purchased. In the dream some of my church members were there with me in the place where we began to
live out the mission to which God had called us.

When I arrived, the church itself was in poor repair,
and the Body of Christ - the congregation - was fragmented and in disorder. The windows were boarded
up; there were no pews or musical instruments; there
were no ushers or hostesses; there was no television
ministry such as we have today. As I walked out in the
midst of the people who were milling around the church
in total disorder, I said, "God, what am I going to
preach? What will I say to these people?" I remember
opening my Bible and looking for some notes to preach,
and God said, "Close your Bible. Son of man, proph-

esy." So I closed my Bible and stood and preached by sheer prophecy for an hour or two.

There were several points that God made through the message He anointed me to preach, and one of the most important points was that **the Body of Christ has been seriously wounded.** In the message that I preached in my dream, I quoted Psalm 41 without even opening my Bible, and when I awoke and looked in the Bible, I found that I had quoted it verbatim.

> *Yea, mine own familiar friend, in whom I trusted, which did eat of my bread, hath lifted up his heel against me. But thou, O Lord, be merciful unto me, and raise me up, that I may requite them. By this I know that thou favorest me, because mine enemy doth not triumph over me. And as for me, thou upholdest me in mine integrity, and settest me before thy face forever. Blessed be the Lord God of Israel from everlasting, and to everlasting. Amen, and Amen. (Psalm 41:9-13)*

In this passage of scripture, we learn where the Body of Christ is wounded. The Body of Christ cannot be wounded from the outside or by the world. Rather it is wounded from within by "...mine own familiar friend," by close and trusted friends. Judas sat at the table with Jesus and Jesus said to him, "Please don't do it, Judas. I identify you and I want you to know that I know who you are and what you're doing. When you dip in this sop with Me, you will identify yourself as that **friend who will betray me.** Please don't do it, Judas." Jesus did not cut Judas off; He created the circumstances where Judas cut himself off. **The Body of Christ is wounded by members of the Body itself.** "Mine own familiar friend, who did sit at the table with me." It is not the world that wounds the Body of Christ - it is we, ourselves, as we war one against the other.

Frustrated religion and worldly legal authority crucified the Lord. The do-gooders and those who went under the guise of "religious" people schemed and connived with Rome - the worldly legal authority - to present facts against Jesus. The facts - legalism - crucified Jesus; it was not the Spirit of truth because that was totally ignored. Nothing but **facts:** finances are in bad shape; church morals appear to be slipping; the building program has stopped. "The fact is...", and the facts do the crucifying and mortally wound the Body of Christ.

But the Spirit of truth far transcends facts. It was a fact that Jesus said, "I am a King." It was a fact that He said, "I will not bow to Rome." But it was **not** a fact that He was trying to destroy God in mankind because Jesus was not a blasphemer. There is such a difference between facts and the Spirit of truth.

In that dream I learned something very important. Chapel Hill Harvester Church was rightly called a City of Refuge, and as a City of Refuge, we have ministered to the injured who have been left dying by the wayside. Many, if not most, of these people came to us from the world, and although some of them remained in the world, many more found refuge within our walls. I am not suggesting that we will no longer be a City of Refuge, but I think there is a broader perspective. God is now calling us to be more than a City of Refuge; He is calling us to become a Balm in Gilead. He is calling us to help heal the Body of Christ. While we will continue to minister as a City of Refuge to those who are pregnant out of wedlock, to those who find themselves trapped in homosexuality, and to those who are bound by drugs and alcohol, that will not be our first call. Our first call now is the healing of the Body of Christ.

Before the miracle working power of God can be manifested, there must come about what I call a "Show Me" faith. That "Show Me" faith is what James talked about when he said, "Even so faith, if it hath not works, is dead, being alone... But wilt thou know, O vain man, that **faith without works is dead?"** (James 2:17,20). "Show Me" faith feeds the hungry and clothes the poor, and that is the level we have now reached - showing our faith by our works. But we must transcend even that to reach a place where we begin to minister on a level never before known by any local congregation on the face of the earth. We must either be a part of this great calling or God will raise up another group of people to do it.

What has brought the wounds to the Body of Christ? Here are some of the normal conclusions that are drawn. "We have differences in doctrine." That is true, but that is not what wounds the Body of Christ. "We have different traditional backgrounds." That is also true, and that may cause schism and bring us into different locations, but it does not bring the mortal wound to the Body of Christ. Another of the causes of the wounded Body of Christ often submitted is that we compare ourselves among ourselves. We say, "We're Baptists and we have 'X' number of members." Or, "We are a local church and this is what we have accomplished."

By pure revelation from the Spirit of God, I submit

that it is not comparison that brings the mortal wound to the Body of Christ. There are differences in structures, such as the Episcopal structure and the congregational structure, and there are different power structures and different organizations. While those differences bring division and walls of partition, they do not mortally wound the Body of Christ. Neither is the wound caused by the fact that we glory in our variety. How many times we have heard that God is a God of variety! That's why He has Baptists, Methodists and Presbyterians, yet because of that concept we are divided.

The wounding of the Body of Christ will be the criterion by which we will finally be judged. At the end of His ministry, Jesus spoke of the final judgment and separation.

> *When the Son of man shall come in his glory, and all the holy angels with him, then shall he sit upon the throne of his glory: And before him shall be gathered all nations: and he shall sepa-rate them one from another, as a shep-herd divideth his sheep from the goats: And he shall set the sheep on his right hand, but the goats on the left. (Mat-thew 25:31-33)*

The nations gathered before Jesus did not begin as goats. Apparently they began as a sheepfold, and while they still retained the look of sheep, in character they had become goats. In the last days, Jesus said, "Beware of false prophets, which come to you **in sheep's clothing** ..." (Matthew 7:15). It would be much too obvious if the goats and the sheep differed in their outward appearance. The difference, therefore, had to be more subtle, such as a difference in character, in the inward man. This separation does not involve the ungodly who are still in the world; this is judgment within the sheepfold itself.

> Then shall the King say unto them on his right hand, Come, ye blessed of my Father, inherit the kingdom prepared for you from the foundation of the world: For I was an hungered, and ye gave me meat: I was thirsty, and ye gave me drink: I was a stranger, and ye took me in: Naked, and ye clothed me: I was sick, and ye visited me: I was in prison, and ye came unto me. Then shall the righteous answer him, saying, Lord, when saw we thee an hungred, and fed thee? or thirsty, and gave thee drink? When saw we thee a stranger, and took thee in? or naked, and clothed thee? Or when saw we thee sick, or in prison, and came unto thee? And the King shall answer and say unto them, Verily I say unto you, Inasmuch as ye have done it unto one of the least of these my brethren, ye have done it unto me. Then shall he say also unto them on the left hand, Depart from me, ye cursed, into everlasting fire, prepared for the devil and his angels: For I was an hungred, and ye gave me no meat: I was thirsty, and ye gave no drink: I was a stranger, and ye took me not in: naked,

and ye clothed me not: sick, and in prison, and ye visited me not. Then shall they also answer him, saying, Lord, when saw we thee an hungred, or athirst, or a stranger, or naked, or sick, or in prison, and did not minister unto thee? Then shall he answer them, saying, Verily I say unto you, Inasmuch as ye did it not to one of the least of these, ye did it not to me. And these shall go away into everlasting punishment: but the righteous into life eternal. (Matthew 25:34-46)

Jesus did not make goats of those whom He separated. They became goats because they took on a goat's character by failing to respond to the needs of those around them.

In God's sheepfold, across the country and around the world, there are those who are hungry for the truth and the Word of God. Yet how many congregations are sleeping on Sunday mornings because of the lack of the pure revelation of God! How many seminaries have dried up and produce nothing for the Kingdom because they are not being fed truth! Those who worship God must worship Him in Spirit and in truth. "I was hungry," Jesus said, "and you gave Me no truth. I was hungry and you bound Me in tradition, but you did not give Me truth." It is important to know that Jesus is not talking about feeding some drunkard walking down the highway who doesn't have anything to eat. That is another gospel altogether. I am talking about feeding **a hunger for pure truth.**

Until we tap the source that produces real truth to

such a degree that God's little ones are not deceived, we have not fed the Body of Christ. "I was thirsty," He said, and how can we separate thirst from the inward fountain? Jesus said, "There shall come **living waters.**" We must hear the cry of the wounded Body of Christ that is thirsty because the waters have not been stirred up. We may feel we can make it from Sunday to Wednesday night, but the living waters are not there to draw from, not even for our own carnalities, much less for the wounded Body of Christ.

We tend to our own businesses, building our own fortresses and feathering our own nests while Jesus says, "I was hungry and thirsty, and you didn't feed Me." We fail to see the Christ in that little soul who struggles to live from one Sunday to the next. We have living waters, but we haven't given them to the ones who need then most. Who are the strangers but those who have been racially segregated, or those who have been mentally segregated, or those who cannot "cut it," as the saying goes, or those who just don't seem to fit?

All my life God has been preparing me for this mission of healing the wounded Body of Christ, and the preparation began when I was very young. When I was a little boy, I used to pass little shanty towns in south Georgia where blacks lived who had never gotten out of slavery. They had simply moved to another place. White folks used to drive from their farms, pick the blacks up, and take them back to the farms to pick cotton and tobacco. One day when I rode with my uncle to pick up some of the black people who lived in those little shanties, I saw little boys and girls naked and almost starving to death. I asked my Uncle Riley, "Why do they live like that?", and he said, "That's their place." When I got home, I said to my mom, "Mom, I don't understand this. I saw something today that I can't close my eyes to. It's bothering me so much that I can't even sleep." After I explained what was troubling me, she said, "Son, you will have to learn that people have got a place."

We think we're such sophisticated people, yet in our minds we've still got people placed. It may not be pleasant to admit, but there are still strangers in the household of faith. Deacons have left this church in the past few months because they thought their little white children were getting too close to little black faces. **This is exactly the judgment that Jesus spoke of between the sheep and the goats!** When someone is made to feel a stranger in the house of God, the judgment of Almighty God has already made the separation.

"I was a stranger in the Christian community and you didn't take time to know who I was." Women have been made strangers in the house of God because we have said, "She's the best **woman** preacher I've ever heard." Why don't we drop the "woman" and say, "She's the best preacher I've ever heard"? We also say, "He's really got soul. He's the best black singer I've ever heard." Why not just drop the "black" and say, "He's the best singer I've ever heard"?

We still have places for people. Everything is all right as long they don't challenge our economic status. It's all right as long they don't try to date our little girls. Oh yes, circumstances will be created in which many people will get up and walk away from the table and never know they have been separated from the Body of Christ.

Naked! Oh, how we have spent our time exposing one another! Noah's sons stood at the tent as Noah lay drunk within, and two of them said, "Don't you know that's a man whom God has spoken to? That's the man to whom God gave the plan to save mankind." Those two sons turned and walked away, saying, "Cover his nakedness. I don't want to see it, and I don't want anyone else to see it either. It's flesh and it's a thorn and it keeps him aware that he's a mortal man, but I don't want to see it, and I will never expose it." But the third son walked in and said, "Ah, I've got a chance to show him. I've got a chance to expose the sins of my father." The same thing was true of Absalom who sat at the gate making friends with the people and saying, "My dad's a busy man, but **I've** got time for you." The book about Oral Roberts and some of the problems in his family was written by a member of Roberts' own staff who had been fired. None other than a member of the Body of Christ wrote the book exposing Kathryn Kuhlman. All the individuals involved in these situations were guilty of uncovering other members of the Body of Christ.

In the last days when the judgment of God is meted out and the goats and sheep are separated, the goats will be those who uncovered their brothers and sisters in the Body of Christ. Personally, I have determined as never before in my life to see the Christ in those around me. While they may flaunt their ungodliness and carnalities in my face, I have determined to look beyond those frailties and say, "If that is a born-again child of God, then somewhere within that flesh man is Christ." I choose, therefore, to see Christ in people and cover all the rest.

"Sick! Not whole, and you didn't minister to me," said Jesus. People are sick in their emotions. They are rejected. They don't want to be rejected. They don't want to be jealous. I've seen those who were born again of the Spirit of God that I knew were still in the sheepfold and oh, how they struggled with jealousy. Shall I cover that jealousy? Shall I visit them in their sickness? Or shall

I cut them off in my mind and say, "I've discerned that you have a demon so get out and go your own way." Or do we say, "No matter what your problems are, I see Christ at work in you, and I'm going to make you well and whole by the way I love you. I'm going to make you whole because the Christ in me sees the Christ in you. I'm not going to turn you loose. I will turn you loose only if you get up and willingly walk away from the table of the Lord."

"I was in prison and you did not come to me," Jesus said. What are the prisons He's talking about? He's talking about the theological prisons that we build for ourselves. We don't know why we believe what we preach because we've never looked at the basis for our beliefs. So we have imprisoned ourselves by what we call theological premises and locked ourselves permanently into prisons of tradition.

Some within the family of God and the sheepfold are imprisoned in marriages. It is the Church's responsibility to hold together what God has joined together. But on the occasions that one of the marriage partners walks away from that covenant relationship, then we, as the Body of Christ, have been the ones who have kept them from full citizenship in the Church. In most churches in the fellowship of God, a divorced person cannot preach the gospel or be ordained, sing in the choir or teach a Sunday school class. Jesus said, "You put Me in a prison and I could never get out of it. I made a mistake and because I could never move away from it, you discounted Me. I was in prison and you never understood Me."

These wounds I am talking about come from **within** the Body of Christ and **within** the sheepfold itself. The shepherd stands at the door of the sheepfold to keep away the wolves and those who try to attack us from the outside. Because the door is well-guarded, we can handle the outside attacks. Therefore, the attacks which mortally wound the Body of Christ will always come from **within** the sheepfold itself. And we have been called to be a healing balm to the wounded Body of Christ.

Another of the subtle wounds inflicted on the Body of Christ is misplaced authority. Judas was capable of being trusted, but he was unable to live up to his capability. The authority he had was not misplaced because Jesus had appointed him; it was misplaced because he failed in the office of trust. Jesus did not make Judas a betrayer. He became one of his own accord, and even Christ Himself could not heal him of it. That is why Judas committed suicide.

There is misplaced authority in the Body of Christ because man has appointed leadership to positions instead of allowing God to call His own leaders.

The internal war among ourselves wounds the Body of Christ. Novices are raised up too soon to ministries they can't handle because bishops and pastors don't have the courage to say, "You're not ready for that yet." Novices being put too quickly into the pulpit without first reaching maturity in the ways of the Holy Spirit can only bring deep wounds to the Body of Christ.

One of the deepest wounds to the Body of Christ has come because we have allowed ourselves to be judged before the eyes and ears of the world. Not long ago I watched one of the most widely viewed Christian television programs in our nation, and essentially it was an hour of expose' against the Body of Christ. As I sat there watching that program, I wept, "God, I see Christ at work in that man and I know he's doing things for the

Kingdom of God, but how can I help him?" Instead of bringing a healing balm to the Body of Christ, he brought nothing more than a deeper cut.

The program dealt with results and statistics from a questionnaire given to different denominational organizations. One of the questions that had been asked was, "Do you believe that Jesus was raised from dead?", and over eighty percent of the Presbyterians, members and pastors included, said no. Another question was, "Was Jesus born of a virgin?" He had a holiday with this one, for most of the pastors had answered that they did not believe in the virgin birth. Two other questions were, "Is Satan real?" and "Is the Bible the Word of God?"

Remember now, the world was listening and judging the credibility and integrity of the Church by what they heard. God forgive us when we allow the world to come inside and look at us! What business is it of theirs how we operate the Kingdom of God? There is just no way the Church can be judged according to the world's standards. The preacher was giving facts, but in doing so, he wounded the Body of Christ because there was no spirit of truth present. Instead of wounding and dividing, we should be saying, "We have brothers who have problems in some of these areas. How can we help them? What are we going to do to restore them? What are we going to do to bring them back?" Facts kill. Truth sets free. "When he, the Spirit of truth, is come, he will guide you into all truth" (John 16:13).

Another wound to the Body of Christ has come because of a breakdown of trust between brethren. Who is my brother? Where can I put my trust? We know that earthly blood brothers will betray us. That is a common occurence, and some of the greatest dramas of all time have been written about how brothers betrayed brothers in the flesh. But what about the family of God? God has joined us together, yet we spend our time betraying each other, breaking trust and destroying confidence with innuendoes and smart little remarks like, "Haven't you noticed? Don't you see his flesh?" How much better it would be to say, "Don't you see the Christ at work in him? Don't you see the spark of the divine in him?" Anyone who even listens to such talk about others is as guilty as those who do the talking, and God will judge them both alike.

Are we going to let people continue to run their mouths about others and to wound the Body of Christ until it finally dies on the face of the earth? We must be part of the solution - the healing - instead of part of the problem.

What can we do? First of all, we must start where we are. How can we heal the Body of Christ in Mississippi or Pennsylvania if we have not healed it with the person who sits beside us in church each Sunday? Do cliques exist within our fellowships? Are we selective about choosing the people we want to associate with? Are we careful to cultivate friendships only among those of our own race? If so, **that** is where the healing must begin! The devil is not going to like it and there will be attacks like we've never seen before. But it will be like water rolling off a duck's back because the Spirit of God is going to cover us in a new dimension and the power of God is going to begin to move.

We must do as the Word of God says and first get the beam out of our own eye. Then God can purge this Body of believers in one local church so we can show the world that we are indeed a lead domino and an example to be followed. If anyone says, "I'm going to marry someone of another race just so I can prove a point," he will probably be lost and go to hell. But if God has joined two people of different races together, their families had better say, "God put them together and this is a spiritual relationship established by God." Then God will take care of the rest.

There are five things we can do to bring healing and to be a Balm of Gilead to the Body of Christ. First, we must begin to intercede at a higher level than we have ever known before. Was it accidental that when Jesus prayed, the prayer he prayed was one of intercession? "Father, heal the Body and **make them one** ." I submit that forked tongues will cease if we spend time on our knees in prayer. When we come out of our prayer closets, we will no longer see anything in others but Jesus Christ, the hope of glory.

This cannot be done by the relatively few people who are called to be intercessors. They will lead us because God has called them to do that. But each and every person must learn that every day when he wakes up, he must say, "God, I'm still here, and I thank You for another day to love somebody. I thank You for another opportunity to be a witness of Your Word."

On a personal note, I was once guilty of saying that I didn't want God to call me to preach. I was a seventeen-year-old boy and I was popular in college. I could have almost anything I wanted. I never tried to date a girl that I couldn't date. I was elected to every office I ever ran for, and then God said, "I want you to preach My Word." At that time I just didn't want to give up the popularity and success I had, so I said "God, I don't want to preach."

But since I made God's will my will, I have been so grateful that God let me preach, and I am so thankful that God called me. I will never again, as long as I live, say, "God, I didn't want to do it." I want to do it. Everything in me wants to do it. Everything in me wants to be able to break down the prisons that have people bound.

The same principle must hold true for you, too, wherever God has placed you. If you do not want to teach Sunday school, then don't prostitute it. If you don't want to sing in that choir, then for God's sake, don't prostitute it. If you don't want to play in the orchestra, please don't prostitute it. If you don't want to be a deacon, then don't prostitute that calling. Your attitude ought to be, "God, I'm so glad I can be a part of what You are doing on the earth."

If God has given you the ability to make money and you have not used that ability for God, then you will see that it will eventually curse you. It will turn on you like a viper. Are you grateful that God gave you two hands to work with? Will you say, "God, I'm so thankful You gave me a sound mind. I'm so grateful that I have a family I can take care of, and I'll see that they've got food and clothing and shelter. But God, I won't give them luxuries at the expense of Your cause, and I'll let You know that You and Your Kingdom are first in my heart."

> *Every man according as he pur-*
> *poseth in his heart, so let him give;*
> *not grudgingly, or of necessity: for God*
> *loveth a cheerful giver. (II Corinthians*
> *9:7)*

That means that every week when you start to work, you will say, "God, You're going to give me the strength to work and I'm going to share it with You. As You prosper me, I won't build bigger barns, but I will say,

'God, Your Kingdom must go forward.' God, I'm Yours and my family is Yours and I'm going to do all I can to help the Kingdom message go forth."

You cannot be a firstfruit to anyone until you understand what I'm saying. We want to **preach** the crucifixion, but we don't want to **experience** it. God cannot use uncrucified people. Until you die to your flesh, your selfishness and greed, and your own selfwill, God can't use you in the Kingdom and you are nothing more than a goat that will finally be separated. But God is long-suffering and I have determined to see the Christ in you, no matter what appearance your flesh gives.

The second thing we can do to bring healing to the wounded Body of Christ is to be the one who reaches out. We're all sitting back, saying, "Why doesn't somebody come minister to me?" Have you ever stopped to realize that God may want **you** to be the one to reach out to someone? Don't sit there and say, "I'm going to wait until someone restores me." There are people who will leave this church, saying, "Nobody came to me." God's not looking for those who are going to wait for someone else to reach out. He's looking for someone who will say, " **I'm** going to be the one to reach out. **I'm** going to be the one to cross over the line."

We draw lines and say, "I want somebody to come over the line to me. I want him to do something for me." Do you understand what I'm saying? **You** be the one to step over the line and say, "God, I'm on the devil's territory and You can use me every day of my life." **You** be the one to bring healing to the Body. **You** be the one to reach out and love somebody. **You** be the one to say, "God, use me." **You** be the one to say, " **I'M THE ONE.** If you need love, I'm the one who will love you. If you need help, I'm the one who will help you. I'll no longer say, 'I receive, I receive'; I'll say, 'I give, I give.' "

The third thing we can do to bring healing to the Body is to help people find their place in the Body of Christ. Many people are wounded because they don't know where they fit. They don't know whether they are a hand, an ear, or a toe. Ephesians 4:12 tells us that the five-fold ministry has been given to perfect the saints, for the work of the ministry, and to edify the Body of Christ - in other words, that they might **mature** the Body and help its members find their place within the Body of Christ.

If you are unsure of your place in the Body, perhaps it is time to ask yourself some questions. Why did God give you an ability in real estate or an education? Why did He give you a talent in music or baking cakes and pies? If you understand the Kingdom, then you know that any ability you have was given by God and belongs to Him. **Those abilities you have are Christ at work within you.** You need to say, "God, take my talents and abilities and do with them whatever you will."

Do you know why God can't prosper you over a long period of time? Some of you have experienced short-term prosperity because Satan knows he is going to destroy you with it. You don't have long-term prosperity bcause you can't be trusted in little things, and God knows that. At one time I wanted to be called a prince of preachers, but no longer. Now I desire only to be called a man of God. When God said to me, "Son of man, prophesy," I said "God, if You will keep my heart open, I'll prophesy and I won't apologize for it. I'll declare it to be the pure Word of God."

The fourth way to bring healing to the Body of Christ is to trust the transcending work of the Holy Spirit. Learn to trust more than anything else the fact that the Holy Spirit transcends any church organization.

The Holy Spirit transcends earthly covenants between a man and a woman. The Holy Spirit transcends **everything** because the Holy Spirit is the transcendent God at work in us. As we learn that the Holy Spirit transcends us and whatever vessels we may be, then we can open ourselves and the glory of God will descend upon us. When that happens, no one will say, "Look what **they** are doing"; they will say, "Look what **God** is doing."

The fifth thing that will bring healing to the Body is finding the source of healing in God's virtue. Before He ascended to His heavenly Father, Jesus told Mary, "You can't touch Me yet." Oh, how she wanted to touch Him. He had saved her from her sins and when she saw that He had risen from the dead, she wanted to touch Him, but He said, "Don't touch Me yet." From that body that she so wanted to touch, she had felt virtue. Like the little woman who had a flow of blood for twelve years and managed to touch the hem of Jesus' garment, she had felt virtue.

The question to be asked of the church locally as well as the church generally across the nation is, "Have we lost our virtue?" Is there no longer healing that comes from the Church when people can say, "Ah, but look at that church. Their members don't fight among themselves. The staff doesn't talk about one another. Oh, they have a place there such as the queen of Sheba saw in Solomon's temple where the people are happy with one another."

Churches have been playing games with the call of God, and virtue has been cut off because of our own doings. God is calling us back to the place to which He originally called us so that virtue can flow once again. Sometimes virtue is in loving arms that can reach out and say, "I'm the only God in the flesh you can touch, but I am God for you." Oh, maybe you won't understand that, and sometimes I fear I'm casting pearls before swine, but perhaps it is something you know by revelation when God says to you, "Share what you have with somebody. Don't hoard it up."

One of the greatest truths I ever learned was not to wait from one Sunday to the next if God gave me a revelation. I have learned to start talking about it wherever and whenever God gives it to me. Just as revelation can cease if it is not shared, virtue dries up if we don't give it away. Unused muscles atrophy and eventually wither and die. Likewise virtue, if kept within, will also die.

One of our pastors recently gave a prophetic message in one of our presbytery meetings in which he said, "God has raised up this church to be a mighty source to the Church universal." In his prophecy he said that God had raised this church up from a broken twig. Now a twig broken from a tree cannot be planted and grow because it has no roots.

Some ten or twelve years ago, I broke the top off a little pine tree and as I placed it in the ground, I said, "Right here, God, is where some things are going to take place. On this property great things will take place for you."

I, too, was a twig broken from a great, great tree, and I loved that tree very much. It was like a mother to me, but I became a stranger in that house. And God said to me, as I lay on my face before Him in Phoenix, Arizona, "I will take your brokenness and I will plant it with roots, and it will grow and it shall become a tree where hundreds shall come night and day. They shall marvel and say, 'Look what the Lord has done.' " Sometimes when I pass by this church at two o'clock in the morning, I see cars on the parking lots and I say, "God, that's the firstfruit, but that's not the end." There will come a time when people will come to this place from all over the world, and they will say, "What has God done in this place?" You may wonder if I'm afraid to say that. No, I'm not, because if everyone in my congregation got up and walked out, I would still say it because God has a people and He will do everything He has said. That very night I got a long distance call from another member of our presbytery who said to me, "Pastor, I would like to submit a scripture to you." And he read,

> *Thus saith the Lord God; I will also take of the highest branch of the high cedar, and will set it; I will crop off the top of his young twigs a tender one, and will plant it upon a high mountain and eminent: In the mountain of the height of Israel will I plant it: and it shall bring forth boughs, and bear fruit, and be a goodly cedar: and under it shall dwell all fowl of every wing; in the shadow of the branches thereof shall they dwell.*
> *(Ezekiel 17:22-23)*

We will build little cottages and we'll say to people who are weary, "Rest with us." In the Spirit I saw some of my brothers who have no pulpits, and God said, "You bring them in and give them shade." I personally don't have money enough to do that, but God is looking for people who will say, "God, take my talents and make money enough through me to do your will." People have done it for their own coffers. Surely there is someone who will say, "God, I don't want to do it for myself anymore. Even if it means that I live in a shanty or a trailer, God, I want to be a part of what You are doing. For after all, I am either going to die or be changed before long anyway."

I want to build a place where I can bring these veterans who have fallen by the wayside because they were weary. I want to care for those who may have gotten out of balance and caused someone to see the flesh man instead of the Spirit man, completely forgetting that they were men to whom God had spoken. God has said, "Don't you touch My anointed." I want to see them healed under the shadow of this great church. You ask if it can be done, and I tell you it is **already** being done. Families are being saved because someone loved them enough to show them they were cared for, although some people would not even give them an extra bedroom to sleep in. We have to put them in hotels and motels, while folks say, "God, I want to do something." Why don't you build an extra room onto your house and tell Chapel Hill that's the church's room and when people need it, they can have it for six months?

I'm not running a popularity contest; I'm building the Kingdom. A man leans back and says, "I've gotten rich, and now I'm going to build a bigger house," while God says, "You fool, I gave that money to you for a purpose; I didn't give it to you for yourself." We have given about $150,000 to Jamaica while our own church owes at least that much also, and people ask, "Pastor, how can you do that? That's not good bookkeeping." Even with the Holy Spirit, they have never understood that what God wants is **not** their money - He wants **them.** Jesus said, "I don't want your money. I want **you** and once I have you, then I'll have everything that belongs to you - your husband, your wife, your children, your house, your car - **everything** you've got becomes Kingdom property."

God wants you to come to His house each Sunday and say, "God, as you have prospered me this week - if it's all of my salary or fifty percent or seventy-five percent - I'll take what I need to live on, and the rest of it is yours." We no longer reserve that kind of giving for special occasions; we give that way every time we come to God's house, and until we learn to do that, we have not understood Kingdom principles at all. The little widow went to the treasury and gave everything she had, which caused Jesus to say,

> *This poor widow hath cast more in,*
> *than all they which have cast into the*
> *treasury: For all they did cast in of their*
> *abundance; but she of her want did cast*
> *in all that she had... (Mark 12:42-44)*

The prophet Elijah went to the house of the widow of Zarephath who was about to starve to death and when he asked for water and bread, she said, "All I have is a handful of meal and a little oil. I'm going to eat with my son, and then we're going to die because we have nothing else." The prophet, his eyes shining with the power of God as it glows in the eyes of an anointed man or woman of God, said, "Give it to me and you will have plenty of oil and plenty of meal." When she asked, "What shall I do?", Elijah said, "You will either trust the prophet of God or you won't" (I Kings 17:8-16). He that hath ears to hear...

Why is there such an attempt to undermine the prophetic voice? Because Satan knows that's the only hope we have for the Kingdom of God. Kingdom people must learn to be like lions let out of the cage for God. If we hear someone attacking the prophecy of God, we ought to be like a chicken on a June bug, saying, "You won't do that here!" The pure Word of God is our whole life and we have no hope if that is gone. The widow gave everything she had, trusting the words of God through the prophet, Elijah. When she went back and opened the meal barrel, she found she had all the meal she needed and her cruse of oil, likewise, was never empty.

Do you know what I'm doing? In my Spirit I'm getting containers ready for the oil of God. What are you doing with your time? Are you working in a shoe store so you can support the Kingdom of God? Or are you working there so you can do something for yourself? You'd better check up and find out, because the eyes of Almighty God are running to and fro, looking for a people He can trust.

How can we bring healing to the Body of Christ? This is the part that won't be popular. **We must learn to be Kingdom givers.** I cannot supply a ministry in Jamaica without funds, and Bishop Benson Idahosa is waiting for cameras in Nigeria. I have letters on my desk pleading for help, but I can't provide that help because some people have never understood Kingdom giving. My heart is full of gentleness, but in the Spirit of God, I'm like a lion. I have brothers and sisters in Haiti, Jamaica, and Africa whom I can't help because we are hoarding up things for ourselves. I cannot build cottages to restore people; I cannot even build a building where we can communicate the Gospel of the Kingdom to the world, to say nothing of a demonstration building God gave me in a vision where people can come and see the work of this church of the Living God in action.

Instead of providing help and fulfilling visions, folk

are saying, "Hey, this is too hard. I'm going to leave while the leaving's good." With the Holy Spirit upon me as a prophet of God, I say as Jesus said to Judas, "What thou doest, do quickly." For God's sake, leave God's table alone. "At My table," Jesus said, "is where I was wounded."

CHAPTER TWO
HEALING IN PROPHETIC MINISTRY

Ultimately, as we have seen, the wounded Body of Christ will lead to the glorified Church. As a local church, God has called us to move past the concept of the "City of Refuge" to the idea of being a "Balm in Gilead." By definition, a balm is a healing, soothing ointment for wounds or an oil for anointing. When the plant or leaf was bruised, it gave forth a salve or a virtue that brought healing.

Jeremiah, the prophet of the Lord, recognized that the Balm in Gilead was symbolic of the ministries of the Church, Jesus Christ, and prophetic teachings when he said, "Is there no balm in Gilead; is there no physician there: why then is not the health of the daughter of my people recovered?" (Jeremiah 8:22). Before the Church of Jesus Christ can become the glorified Church and enter into its rightful place of ruling and reigning with Christ, a healing must take place from within the Church itself, and that healing will come as a soothing balm upon those who are wounded.

God has called us to be that healing balm to the Body of Christ, and I believe, as a part of that ministry, a prophetic voice is required. How does a prophet or a prophetic church fit into God's design for providing a healing balm for the Body of Christ? We know that before Jesus Christ can return to the earth, the Church must achieve the unity of the faith, but I believe that even before unity can take place, the Body of Christ must be healed.

There is healing in the prophetic voice. At times that voice may cut as deeply as a surgeon's knife as it admonishes and cleanses, but it will ultimately bring

27

healing. As we read in Proverbs 18:21, "Death and life are in the power of the tongue: and they that love it shall eat the fruit thereof." The tongue has the power of life, cleansing, wholeness and healing as it brings us God's presence and direction.

Paul's letter to the Hebrews reminds us that the Word of God is powerful and able to cut us to the very quick of our inward man. It discerns our innermost parts and through that discernment, it brings healing.

> For the word of God is quick, and powerful, and sharper than any two-edged sword, piercing even to the dividing asunder of soul and spirit, and of the joints and marrow, and is a **discerner of the thoughts and intents of the heart.** (Hebrews 4:12)

As we speak prophetically, from the voice of God's prophet comes healing.

In Matthew's account of the centurion who sought healing for his servant, we find that the centurion knew the meaning of being under authority as he said to Jesus, "Speak the word only, and my servant shall be healed" (Matthew 8:8). In the same way - through prophetic words - healing comes to the Body of Christ.

Even Jesus Himself said that the words He spoke brought healing and an abundant life. And whether it be one single voice crying in the wilderness or a prophetic Church that God has placed in His Body, the prophetic words they utter bring healing to the Body of Christ.

Prophetic words are referred to as words of reconciliation (II Corinthians 5:19), or words that bring us together and cause us to forget our differences. There are no differences that exist between members of the Body of Christ that could not be reconciled by the Balm of Gilead, if we would only allow it to do its work. The power of the Holy Spirit could so cut away the putrefaction that the Body could be purified and healing could take place. But we have closed ourselves off from the Word of God because we are afraid of what He might say to us. We are afraid that God might just **make** us make things right with those around us. We must give ourselves freely into the hands of God before He can do His healing work within us, either individually or collectively as His corporate Body on earth.

The prophetic tongue sets free by speaking the truths of God. Jesus said, "Ye shall know the truth, and the truth shall make you free" (John 8:32). Truth is the prophetic voice of God, and it can save a life by providing correction at the time when it is most needed. The Apostle Paul said of this correction,

> *Now no chastening for the present seemeth to be joyous, but grievous: nevertheless afterward it yieldeth the peaceable fruit of righteousness unto them which are exercised [trained] thereby. (Hebrews 12:11)*

Although they may seem hard at the time, words of correction direct our course and guide us as we move through this life. Words of correction bring reconciliation as God speaks in the flesh.

How else will God speak today other than by written revelation and prophetic voices? Anointed teachers of God break these revelations down so the people of God can understand them, but prophetic voices of God must take the lead and speak **as God in the flesh.** In I Peter 2:2, Peter refers to this as "...the sincere [pure] milk of the word," which brings life, direction and healing.

For this reason, God has placed in the Church not only apostles, who establish new works of God under His anointed direction, but prophets. And what good is a prophet if he does not prophesy? Why have a prophetic voice if it does no more than teach what has already been revealed and taught? It is not prophecy to teach what has already been prophesied. Prophecy opens us to new revelation, insight and dimension. It cuts where cutting has never before taken place. It moves us to areas where we've never moved before. Before the Church can become the glorified Church God is waiting for, our ears must be opened to hear prophetic words of God.

God places in the Church pastors and teachers who take the prophetic word and make it known to the Body of Christ on a level which they can understand. The word must be given so that a six-year-old can understand it, as well as a sixteen-year-old and a sixty-year-old. That is the reason for Sunday School, Children's Church, and youth ministries, and if they miss their calling, they have no right to exist. They break down to appropriate levels what God is saying prophetically through the voice of Christ to the Church.

God sends out evangelists to carry to the world the blessings they have heard from the Word of God and through the mouths of the prophets. With the authority given by God, they preach messages that bring people into the presence and glory of Jesus Christ.

I Corinthians 12 reminds us that God has placed within the Church not only prophets but also the gift of prophecy, and there is a difference. The **gift** of prophecy may come upon anyone in the Body of Christ who is Spirit-filled, and their prophecy must be judged by the elders present. There is no judging by elders of the **voice of the prophet** if he or she is God's called-out man or woman who speaks as a prophet. If he is called as a prophet, there is no need for judging or proof because his ministry must prove itself.

The prophetic utterances that come from among members of the congregation as a gift must be judged to see if indeed God has spoken. It is a beautiful sight to see prophetic voices begin to speak out in a Spirit-filled congregation and the way in which the rest of the Body becomes attentive as God speaks through His vessels. But that in no way diminishes the fact that God must have prophets and prophetic churches in these last days to bring healing and direction to the Body of Christ. Being one of those prophetic churches is a truly awesome call of God.

In the fifth chapter of I Thessalonians there is direction concerning the last days. The Apostle Paul says that the last days should not take us by surprise because we, as the children of light, should know the signs of the end times.

> *But ye, brethren, are not in darkness, that that day should overtake you as a thief. Ye are all the children of the light, and the children of the day: we are not of the night, nor of darkness. Therefore let us not sleep, as do others; but let us watch and be sober. (I Thessalonians 5:4-6)*

Further along in this same chapter, Paul gives specific

instructions about things we are to do (I Thessalonians
5:12-23). The one verse I especially wish to emphasize
is verse 20 in which Paul says, "Despise not prophesyings." **Despise not prophesyings,** for in the last days
prophecy will be the means by which God directs His
Church.

There are a few points I wish to make concerning a
prophet which will apply not only to an individual
prophet but also to prophetic ministries and to churches
that are prophetic in the historicity of God. Not every
church is under the same charge, challenge, or reward
as those churches which God has set in a position of
prophecy.

First, it is important to know that a prophet's own
ministry must prove itself. Again I reemphasize that this
is not the same as the gift of prophecy that God has
placed within the Church in which the elders must sit in
judgment. In directing Israel, which is a forerunner of
the Church of Jesus Christ, it was written,

> *If there arise among you a prophet,*
> *or a dreamer of dreams, and giveth thee*
> *a sign or a wonder, And the sign or the*
> *wonder come to pass, whereof he*
> *spake unto thee, saying, Let us go after*
> *other gods, which thou hast not known,*
> *and let us serve them; Thou shalt not*
> *hearken unto the words of that prophet,*
> *or that dreamer of dreams: for the Lord*
> *your God proveth you, to know*
> *whether ye love the Lord your God with*
> *all your heart and with all your soul.*
>
> *Ye shall walk after the Lord your*

> *God, and fear him, and keep his com-*
> *mandments, and obey his voice, and ye*
> *shall serve him, and cleave unto him.*
>
> *And that prophet, or that dreamer of*
> *dreams, shall be put to death; because*
> *he hath spoken to turn you away from*
> *the Lord your God, which brought you*
> *out of the land of Egypt, and redeemed*
> *you out of the house of bondage, to*
> *thrust thee out of the way which the*
> *Lord thy God commanded thee to walk*
> *in. So shalt thou put the evil away from*
> *the midst of thee. (Deuteronomy*
> *13:1-5)*

Just as there were in those days, so today also there are both legitimate prophets and false prophets. It is essential that we understand that for every reality of God, there is a counterfeit of Satan which cannot be discerned with the natural senses. Telling the difference requires spiritual discernment from the altars of the Almighty God.

The Old Testament writer said that false prophets would come. Sometimes God permits them to test us so He can discover our level of spiritual discernment. We are about to enter into the period of the greatest deception ever known to the Christian Church, and without spiritual discernment there will be many, even those whom we call "the very elect," who will be led down the path that will eventually lead to total destruction and devastation.

If a prophet comes who attempts to lead us away from truths established by revelation from the Word of

God and its power, Spirit and character, he is a false prophet. But we do not need to worry about dealing with him because God already has a plan for taking care of him (verse 5) - **"that prophet...shall be put to death."** God will not suffer false teachings if the congregation remains in a spiritual posture before Him. He will unmask false prophets who may come among us, but that requires that we maintain a high level of spiritual discernment which can only come through the practice of spirituality.

It is important to know that a prophet of God or a prophetic church is under the blessing of God. I Chronicles 16:22 says, "Touch not mine anointed, and do my prophets no harm." When God spoke of blessing those who bless Israel, I believe that was a foreshadowing of what was to come in these times. I believe He was speaking of those who bless not only His Church but also those within the Church who are on the front lines of ministry. I believe the day will come when God will bless those who understand the role of a prophet and by discernment know the difference between the man and the message which is anointed of God; who knows the difference between the vessel and the one whom God has called out to speak His messages with power to this generation.

Although prophetic ministries are under the blessing of God, it is important to know that such ministries are not usually honored among their own families. Some of those who are involved with these ministries will be rejected by those closest to them and will be called fools. They will be called "odd" and "strange." Prophetic ministers have always and shall always be that way.

Jesus Himself was thought strange and was even rejected among His own family who tried to distract

Him from His prophetic ministry and put Him in the cares of life. He finally had to say, "Who is My mother? And who are My brethren?"

> And it came to pass, that when Jesus had finished these parables, he departed thence. And when he was come into **his own country,** he taught them in their synagogue, insomuch that they were astonished, and said, Whence hath this man this wisdom, and these mighty works? **Is this not the carpenter's son?** is not his mother called Mary? and his brethren, James, and Joses, and Simon, and Judas? And so his sisters, are they not all with us? Whence then hath this man all these things?

> And they were offended in him. But Jesus said unto them, **A prophet is not without honour, save in his own country, and in his own house.** And he did not many mighty works there **because of their unbelief.** (Matthew 13:53-58)

Those who heard Jesus teaching in the synagogue could not understand how Jesus could be so different from all His brothers and sisters. "Is this not the carpenter's son? Why does He have all this power and they have none?" **It is always Satan's intention to bring a prophetic voice down to a natural level.** That is why the most devastating attacks against a prophetic ministry come from those who are closest to the prophet, from those who have sat at his table and who know him best. Such attacks always mortally wound the Body of Christ.

A prophet is not without honor except in his own country where he has a degree of familiarity with the people who see him as a man or a woman instead of as an oracle of God. This scripture is so important that it deserves a dual witness, and the gospel writer Mark recorded it also in his gospel (6:1-5). This explains why even today a prophet of God often goes no further than laying his hands on a few people and healing them. Because of familiarity, the people surrounding him fail to see that he is a called prophet of God and that he is the **only** means God has of communicating to the world today.

The prophet is not **a** method that God uses, but in fact is the **only** method He uses to speak to this generation. The prophet is God's only method of informing this generation of new and greater revelation. Who will speak to this generation if God does not raise up prophets to do so? In the Gospel of Luke we read,

> *And he began to say unto them, This day is the scripture fulfilled in your ears. And all bare him witness, and wondered at the gracious words which proceeded out of His mouth. And they said, Is not this Joseph's son?' (Luke 4:21-22)*

This time they said, "Is not this **Joseph's** son?" They no longer spoke of Him as Mary's son who joined with the Holy Spirit. They brought it to an even lower level when they spoke of Him as being the son of a mortal man because they denied the virgin birth. Then Jesus said to them, "Ye will surely say unto me this proverb, Physician, heal thyself."

Jesus knew that one day they would see Him hanging on a cross and that many times they would see Him weary after trying days. He knew also that He would not be accepted in His own country.

There is another aspect, however, to the prophetic word. Even though a prophet may be respected and honored, he can do nothing unless there are anointed ears to hear what he says. In the story of Naaman's healing, there were other lepers in addition to him, but they were not healed because they did not hear and accept the prophetic word of God as Naaman did. He was healed because he dared to be tested of God until he heard with anointed ears and went and dipped himself in the River Jordan seven times.

God is waiting for a people with anointed ears who will not miss His opportunities and who stand ready and willing to be used of Him. Just as it is necessary for a prophetic church to have a prophet, it is also necessary for a prophetic church to have people whose ears are anointed.

There is a price to be paid for being a prophet or for being a prophetic church. God told me that I would be persecuted and that this church would be persecuted as well, and that will prove true ten times out of ten in every prophetic ministry that God raises up.

This persecution will not always come from outside the church. When strife and persecution take place from within the Body, spiritual people must learn how to respond instead of react. I remember when I was growing up I was raised to believe that dancing was the gateway to hell itself. Who put dancing in our feet in the first place? God did. The devil has prostituted it, but it was God who put it there originally.

I was driving downtown the other day and as I stopped at a red light, I looked over and noticed a young man about ten years old standing on the corner. As I watched him, he suddenly began to dance and move like I've never seen before, and I wondered what in the world was going on. Then I noticed that he had little earphones in his ears and was apparently listening to music. That music must have gotten so good that he just had to dance! And when God gets good enough in us, our feet will begin to show it, too.

Believe me, we have been persecuted from both within and without about our beliefs concerning dancing in the Church. But that does not bother us because we are a prophetic church and we are in the process of learning how to respond to these criticisms instead of react to them. We are not going to change one thing that we believe God has told us to do in this ministry because of criticism and persecution, no matter where it comes from.

Chapel Hill Harvester Church is a prophetic ministry raised up of God for several reasons. One of those reasons is that we are to become a healing influence in the Church universal through the pure word of prophecy. The wounded Body of Christ must undergo spiritual surgery before it can be healed. All foreign matter must be removed and God must purge and cleanse our congregation. Then we will be healed and be able to share this healing with other congregations by demonstrating to them the things that God has told us. One day those who have spoken against us and our ministry will need us and need the things we have. They will need

God to heal and purge them, and when they do, we will be here with our arms open to them, even though they have spoken against us. That is what a prophetic church is all about.

My father and mother both received the baptism of the Holy Spirit at an early age during the first move of God's Holy Spirit in this nation. Because of the baptism, my father was disassociated from the Baptist Church, and he began to preach wherever doors were opened, many times outside under brush arbors. He often had threats made on his life, and once he was actually held at gunpoint. God called my dad to be a prophetic voice, and he was persecuted then just as we are today. But that did not stop him. He went on to become a great man of God in Pentecostal circles and with the Lord's help, won many thousands of souls to God. Because God always protected my father, no harm ever came to him as he went about doing the work of the Lord.

Today we are also on the cutting edge of what God is doing in the world. We have entered Satan's territory and the time for playing games is over. Satan is attacking us in ways we never dreamed possible, but he cannot stop us. The victory has already been won through Jesus Christ.

Another man who was persecuted because he was on Satan's territory was Martin Luther King, Jr. I believe that the man was a prophet of God and that he started a great move of God in this country. When I first heard about his work, I publicly supported it from my pulpit. My brother Don and I signed a manifesto, along with him and his father, Daddy King (Martin Luther King, Sr.), which stated that we would not bow to civil authority in racial matters because we believed that civil authority was wrong and that laws bringing about segregation of whites and blacks were not of God.

What finally happened to Martin Luther King, Jr.? He was stabbed several times. He had bombs thrown on his porch. He was jeered and mocked and threatened and finally killed. Why? Because the man was a prophet of God.

Martin Luther King, Jr. was a dreamer. He had a dream that some day boys and girls and people of all races would be able to walk down the streets holding hands and loving God together. He was a dreamer and his brothers did not like him. Who killed this man? The world did not kill him. Religious fanatics killed him because of what he stood for. We are finding out now that religious fanatics will hurt the cause of God in these last days also, and we must remember that prophets of God are always persecuted by those within.

There are four responsibilities that a prophet or a prophetic ministry has when they know they have been called of God. **First of all, a prophet must know who he is in God.** He cannot depend on anyone else to identify him. He must know before the altars of Almighty God that his calling is legitimate. Jesus knew who He was, and He knew the work He was sent to do. A prophet must know who he is with such conviction that neither all the devils in hell nor persecution from within the Body of Christ can shake him.

The second thing a prophet must do is let God handle his persecutors. God has taught me that lesson personally. We must not fret because of evil doers, and we must always try to see the Christ in our brother, no matter how small it may be. We must love our persecutors in spite of themselves, accepting them as brothers and sisters and standing in the gap for them. If we fail to do that, we will no longer be a prophetic ministry.

Thirdly, a prophet must remember that his brethren are also a part of the household of faith. Even if they become critical and bring persecution against us, God still loves them, and God has called us to reach a higher dimension than they. He has called us to a ministry that inevitably involves persecution, and part of learning to deal with it is learning to overcome our negative feelings about our persecutors and love them as He does. We are called to love the unlovable.

Fourthly and finally, we must learn how to rejoice in the midst of our trials. The Book of Revelation tells us that we are victorious, no matter what trials beset us, and that assurance enables us to stand fast among our persecutors. We must learn how to follow the Holy Spirit during hard and difficult times. If we learn how to flow with the Spirit life and in the calling God has given us, we will find that He will never, never fail us.

CHAPTER THREE
THE PRIESTHOOD AND LORDSHIP OF JESUS

To become the glorified Church that God intends for us to become, healing must take place beginning in each of us individually. This begins a chain reaction of sorts because this healing, cleansing flow will move from individual to individual. Then it will move into the local congregation, and from there it will move from congregation to congregation, nation to nation, and continent to continent. We must become sensitive to the fact that the wounded Body of Christ must, in fact, be healed. Before we can mature and be that which God has called us to be, there must be both inner healing and outer healing.

As we have seen, the Body of Christ is indeed wounded. It has been wounded by misunderstandings about the placement of males and females in the Body, by abused authority, and by leaders who dare to judge each other and air their problems and differences before a world which stands ready to receive the words that they speak against each other.

Surprisingly, some of the greatest enemies of our great national ministries today are not outsiders or unbelievers. The attacks from so-called "fellow members" of the Body of Christ have not only broken down trust in leadership but also wounded the Body of Christ.

God now wants to restore His Church and bring it to a higher level than ever before, but it must all begin with individual healings.

Sometimes healing is not pleasant when it is taking place. Peter said, "That which for a moment seems to be a burden to us works for us a more exceeding reward." The prophetic Word of God cuts as a surgeon's knife to purify us and to make us strong, and until this healing takes place, we cannot enter into   or understand the priesthood and Lordship of Jesus Christ.

How does the priesthood and Lordship of Jesus bring healing to the wounded Body of Christ? Because the Body of Christ is wounded, it must be healed itself before it can touch the world. An interesting story is recorded in John's gospel which gives us insight into the healing that must take place and the way in which it affects our witness to the world.

> *But Mary stood by outside the sepulchre weeping. And as she wept she stooped down and looked into the sepulchre and seeth two angels in white sitting, the one at the head and the other at the feet, where the body of Jesus had lain. And they say unto her, Woman, why weepest thou? And she saith unto them, Because they have taken away my Lord and I know not where they have lain him.*

> *And when she had thus said, she turned herself back and saw Jesus standing and knew not that it was Jesus. And Jesus saith unto her, Woman, why weepest thou? and whom seeketh thou? She, supposing him to be the gardener, said, Sir, if thou have borne him hence, tell me where thou hast laid him and I will take him away. (John 20:11-15)*

Mary thought Jesus was the gardener, and that is very significant. Even today, the divinity and the anointing of God that work so mightily in His Church are often taken to be something far less. But when Jesus called her name, suddenly Mary's eyes were opened and she realized who He was. When she realized that this was her Master, her first impulse was to reach out and touch Him. But He told her not to touch Him because He had not yet ascended to His Father. He also told her to go to the brethren and tell them that He would be ascending to His and their Heavenly Father.

Let us notice the setting here. Mary is in the garden and is very troubled because she does not understand what has taken place. It is significant that she was looking for the body. Instead of looking for the resurrected Christ, she was looking for the dead body. Many people in religious circles spend their time looking for old religious artifacts instead of looking for a risen, living power within themselves and within those to whom they minister. The world is not looking for death because they see enough of that every day. The world is looking for life and for something greater than they have ever known before.

Now why did Jesus tell Mary not to touch Him until He had ascended to the Father? I believe it is because God first had to approve the sacrifice that Jesus had made. The Father had to say, "Well done, Son." Jesus first had to gain approval from His father, and until we have the approval of the Father, the Church of Jesus Christ cannot touch the world. Until the Father has deemed us a Church without spot or wrinkle and has approved our sacrifice, we cannot rule and reign with Him.

When Jesus had gained approval from the Father, He did not return as a priest - He returned as a Lord. He returned as an authority figure, as one who had been with the Father and had been released by the Father to come and touch the world. When Jesus returned from the Father, He no longer forbade people to touch Him. He told Thomas not only to touch Him, but to thrust his hand into His side to make sure He was real. The Church needs to reach the place where we are so in touch with the Father, and so approved by the Father that we can say to the world, "Thrust your hands into our side and see if we are not real. See if there is not the spirit of truth among us. See if there is not genuine healing power among us. See if we do not have valid solutions to people's problems."

Jesus had to be touched first with the feelings of our infirmities and become a priest unto us to such a degree that God could approve what He did. We must also be approved of by the Father. We must do what He has called us to do, not what we **think** He has called us to do or what He has called someone else to do. This suggests a relationship with Him. Over and over again Jesus said, "I cannot speak unless the Father speaks something through me. His words are Mine and My words are His." I believe the hour has come for the Church to be just that in tune with God. But we can never do it by righteous works, no matter how hard we try. We must understand that as the Body of Christ on this earth, we take on His righteousness.

In John 17 we read the words of Jesus as He says,

I have glorified thee on the earth: I have finished the work which thou gavest me to do. And now, O Father,

glorify thou me with thine own self with
the glory which I had with thee before
the world was. (John 17:4-5)

Notice that He said He had finished the work that God had given Him to do. What has God given you to do that will let you stand up and say, "I'm the one, God. You can count on me to do what You have given me to do and I'll not try to do what You have given someone else to do."

When Jesus ascended to His Father, He had completed the full circle. He started with the Father, and the Father sent Him out on a mission of incarnation. Now He has returned to the Father to receive the same glory that He had before. I believe the Church, though wounded and fragmented and diseased, must also reach the place, after it has been touched with infirmity and has felt the pain of the world, where such approval has been given of the Father that we speak, act and move with the self-same authority that Jesus had. For Jesus Himself said, "Even as I have been in the world, now you are in the world." We are, after all, nothing but His embodiment here on earth. And when we have His authority, the wounded Body will become the glorified Body of Christ.

Only when the wounded Body becomes the glorified Body can we reach out to the world and say, "Now we can touch you and change you, because we have a new authority from our Heavenly Father. He has approved our glorification." That is a new revelation and concept.

I have manifested thy name unto the
men whom thou gavest me out of the
world: thine they were, and thou gavest

> *them to me; and they have kept thy*
> *word. (John 17:6)*

Those of us who are pastors must understand that God gives people to us and He is the one who adds to the Church. We must not claim these people as our own. We must always know they are a gift from God to us to be cared for very tenderly.

> *Now they have known that all things*
> *whatever thou hast given me are of*
> *thee. For I have given unto them the*
> *words thou gavest me; and they have*
> *received them, and have known surely*
> *that I came out from thee, and they*
> *have believed that thou didst send me.*
> *(John 17:7-8)*

It is so very important for the world to know that we have come out from God. Until they know that the Body of Christ is genuine, we are crying in vain. They have to know that it is God who sent us and not we ourselves. God is love and life, and that is exactly what the world is seeking, whether they realize it or not.

> *I pray for them: I pray not for the*
> *world, but for them which thou hast*
> *given me; for they are thine. And all*
> *mine are thine, and thine are mine; and*
> *I am glorified in them.*

> *And now I am no more in the world*
> *but these are in the world, and I come to*
> *thee. Holy Father, keep through thine*

> *own name those whom thou hast given*
> *me, that they may be one as we are.*
> *(John 17:9-11)*

Now when Jesus prayed this prayer we assume that His physical body was still on the earth. But I believe that this is the prayer He prayed to the Father in that hour after His ascension.

> *While I was with them in the world, I*
> *kept them in thy name: those that thou*
> *gavest me I have kept, and none of*
> *them is lost, but the son of perdition;*
> *that the scripture might be fulfilled. Now*
> *come I to thee; and these things I speak*
> *in the world, that they might have my*
> *joy fulfilled in themselves. I have given*
> *them thy word; and the world hath*
> *hated them, because they are not of the*
> *world, even as I am not of the world.*

> *I pray not that thou shouldest take*
> *them out of the world, but that thou*
> *shouldest keep them from the evil.*
> *They are not of the world, even as I am*
> *not of the world. Sanctify them through*
> *thy truth: thy word is truth.   (John*
> *17:12-17)*

After these words are spoken, a very challenging turn takes place as Jesus turns His attention from His mission to the commission He gives us.

> *As thou has sent me into the world,*

even so have I also sent them into the
world. And for their sakes I sanctify
myself, that they also may be sanctified
through the truth. Neither pray I for
these alone, but for them also which
shall believe on me through their word;
That they all may be one; as thou,
Father, art in me, and I in thee, that
they also may be one in us: that the
world may believe that thou hast
sent me. *(John 17:18-21)*

Now notice that key point at the end. In the well-
being and unity of the wounded Body of Christ, the
Father and the Son and the Church are one. Because of
that unity and well-being, Jesus says, the world will
believe. There must be that oneness of the Father, Son,
Spirit and Body of Christ before the world will believe
that we, the Body, are truly a part God's divine plan.
The world has to believe as much in the Church today
as they believed in Jesus in His day. Perhaps Jesus'
words will take on new meaning now: "Greater works
than these shall he do; because I go unto my Father"
(John 14:12).

The first requirement of the glorified Church is unity
with the Father, Son, and Holy Ghost, and I believe that
God is giving us, through the Spirit, the things we need
to meet this requirement. Only when we meet this
requirement can we go out and touch the world,
because only then will they believe we are who we say
we are.

If the world touches us in our impurity, we must
remind them that we are but symbols of that victory to
come. We are but symbols of God's righteousness until

we literally **become** the righteousness of Christ. And I believe that God is calling us to a new level. Jesus was God in the flesh, and even as He was in the world, so must we be in the world, and even greater. That which is impure within us must be cleansed and removed.

I am not saying that the flesh life will disappear, but that the Body will be able to tell the difference between Spirit and flesh. Those who move too far away from the natural man become no good to God in the Spirit, and those who move too far from the spiritual man will lose their unity with God. A fine balance must be found, and the Holy Spirit will cause each and every person who is open to Him to find that balance.

As we recognize our flesh and find our righteousness, not in our flesh man but in our spirit, we become the manifest sons of God. Only when the Body is purified and glorified can we take on the likeness of Christ in its totality. That is when the Church shall be changed in a moment, in the twinkling of an eye, and become the great glorified Church of Christ on the earth.

Everything that the Church will do, Christ has already done. We are living out the same experiences that He did. There is a passage of scripture that shows us just where we are in prophecy at the present time.

> And when it was evening, his disciples came to him, saying, This is a desert place, and the time is now past; send the multitude away, that they may go into the villages, and buy themselves victuals [food]. (Matthew 14:15)

When this scripture is related to Matthew 9:38, the scripture on which this church was founded, we then

know just what Chapel Hill Harvester Church and the
Harvester ministry is all about. Jesus said,

> *Pray ye therefore the Lord of the har-*
> *vest, that he will send forth labourers*
> *into his harvest. (Matthew 9:38)*

The disciples told Jesus to send the multitudes away so
they could buy food for themselves. That is very significant because their attitude was, "Let the people do it for
themselves".

But Jesus said to them, "They need not depart. **You**
give them to eat." Now what fits in right there? **"I'm the
one."** The disciples were the ones to do it then, and we
are the ones to do it now. All the disciples had was five
loaves and two fishes. We started small also, but when
we give all that we have, Jesus has a way of multiplying it
and making more than enough for the multitudes so
that there is even an overflow.

So many comparisons can be made between this
parable and the day in which we live. There was, in that
day, a hungry multitude. Today, there is a hungry world
in a desert place. They are void of normal emotions,
void of right attitudes, void of beneficial and proper
relationships, and they are waiting and longing to be
touched by someone who has the answer.

Also, as in this parable, the disciples had an attitude of
letting the people fend for themselves, and today,
although many people know that there is a dying world
out there, their attitude is still, "Let someone else do it."
They see the problems and still don't want to do anything about it themselves. But I believe that God is
putting in the hearts and spirits of some people today
the desire to be the ones to make some changes. He is

putting in the hearts of His people the desire to be the ones used of Him.

I believe the five loaves that Jesus used represent the five-fold ministry He left to His Church. When Jesus returned from the captivity of hell, He gave to the Church apostles, prophets, pastors, teachers and evangelists, the ministries that feed the Body of Christ. Everyone cannot be an apostle. Everyone cannot be a prophet. There are apostolic churches, prophetic churches and teaching churches. We need to realize that we all have different callings, but when we all work together, there is more than enough food for the world. God is raising up people all over the world to work together to establish His Kingdom, and it takes all these ministries united to become the glorified Church Universal.

The wounded Body of Christ will become well when ministries stop warring one another and unite in support of each other. Then and only then can we reach the world for Jesus Christ and establish, once and for all time, God's Kingdom on the earth.

CHAPTER FOUR
THE TABLE OF THE LORD

We have learned, as the Church of the Lord Jesus Christ, that we are in the process of bringing Christ back to crown Him King of kings and Lord of lords. In order for this to happen, we must be a worthy Bride who is mature, able to discern, empowered by the Holy Spirit, and sensitive to her mission upon the earth. Until the wounded and fragmented Body of Christ is made well and brought into a unity of purpose, Christ cannot come again. We need not wonder **if** He will come back or not; He cannot. Christ can only return when the people of God have reached that place of unity in which the Spirit and the Bride can say, "Come." Only then will we experience the coming of Christ and answer the prayer which Jesus prayed in the seventeenth chapter of John when He said, "Father, I pray not that You take them out of the world, but that You prepare them and keep them in the world." God will not leave this planet uninhabited.

God's desire and plan is that the whole earth should again be filled with His glory, and you and I are God's instruments to bring that plan to pass. John the Revelator was not speaking merely words when he said, "The kingdoms of this world shall become the Kingdom of our God." No other institution shall bring God's Kingdom to pass on this earth except the Church - vibrant, alive, and empowered, knowing who she is, and knowing she can stand on the very toes of death and challenge it as the last enemy to be conquered.

A worthy Bride is one who is hungry for truth and thirsty for the Spirit of God. She must understand that many people have been made strangers because of racial prejudice and because the role of women in the Church has not been understood. She must understand that the Body of Christ is now fragmented and that she is instrumental in its healing so the Church can touch the world as God intends.

God's ultimate goal is to establish His rule again upon the earth. Many people would say that the purpose of God is to save every creature on the earth, and I believe that salvation was God's ultimate intention. But His goal now is to restore order in the universe. Satan lifted himself up against the authority of God and caused disunity in the universe. And now the purpose of God's Church is to restore the earth to its rightful owner - God.

Before the world will know a strong Church and a worthy Bride, the Church must undergo purging so that it can become whole and unified. As long as Christians cannot sit at the table of the Lord together, whether we be Pentecostals, Catholics, or Episcopalians; if we cannot sit at the table of the Lord in unity and discern the Body of Christ together, there is no way that Christ can come again or that the Church can be properly prepared as His Bride. Therefore, to accomplish His goal, God must find ways of purging His Body to bring not only unity on the one hand, but separation on the other.

When I speak of separation, be assured that it is not God's will that anyone be cut off. On the contrary, God wills that all come to repentance. Also be assured, however, that we are the ones who separate ourselves. God sets the circumstances, but we bring about the separation. Although God wants everyone to become a part of His plan, each person must make the decision for himself.

Likewise also these filthy dreamers

> *defile the flesh, despise dominion*
> *[authority], and speak evil of dignities*
> *[majesty]. (Jude 8)*

How does judgment take place at the table of the Lord? Here is the criterion. This passage of scripture tells us that these people despised control (dominion, authority). Their spirits were not the Spirit of God; they had religious spirits, and spirits just like that are being manifested in these last days.

> *But, beloved, remember ye the*
> *words which were spoken before of the*
> *apostles of our Lord Jesus Christ; How*
> *that they told you there should be*
> *mockers in the last time, who should*
> *walk after their own ungodly lusts.*
> *These be they who separate them-*
> *selves, sensual, having not the Spirit.*
> *(Jude 17-19)*

We find three biblical examples of people with such spirits who separated themselves from the people of God.

> *Woe unto them! for they have gone*
> *in the way of Cain, and ran greedily*
> *after the error of Balaam for reward,*
> *and perished in the gainsaying of Core*
> *[Korah]. (Jude 11)*

The way of Cain was doing things his own way, by the mind of reason rather than by the blood redemption that God wanted (Genesis 4:3-5). Cain said, "Why should I bring a lamb to sacrifice as a firstfruit? I will simply bring the largest orange I have or the finest apple or cucumber or tangerine and give it to God because my mind of reason tells me I know God better than He knows Himself." We cannot discern the things of God by the mind of reason. We must discern by the Spirit of truth.

Balaam assumed, by his mind of reason, doctrine, and theory, that a righteous God would estrange Himself from a rebellious Israel. He failed to understand, however, the grace and mercy of God.

Korah denied that God dwelled in the flesh of Moses. Some people today have so rejected the idea of "God in the flesh" that they don't even realize that the main characteristic of the spirit of the antichrist is its denial of the Incarnation. Until we can love those we have seen in the flesh, we cannot truly love God. By the same criterion, until we recognize God's authority in the flesh, we will never see God.

Understanding those two statements allows us to understand spiritual authority. Some have considered spiritual authority as a tremendous threat, when it is actually God's way of bringing restoration.

We are told to judge the sin of Korah for there will be a denial of spiritual authority in these last days. God's redemption rests in the blood of Jesus Christ and not in the works of righteousness, as Balaam thought. And we must not be led by the mind of reason as Cain was. We must understand that God did not separate these three individuals from the Body. He created the circumstances in which they judged themselves and chose to walk away from God's table, either defiled, deceived, or justified.

But Israel, which followed after the

> *law of righteousness, hath not attained*
> *the law of righteousness. Wherefore?*
> *Because they sought it not by faith, but*
> *as it were by the works of the law. For*
> *they stumbled at that stumblingstone;*
> *As it is written, Behold, I lay in Sion a*
> *stumblingstone and rock of offence:*
> *and whosoever believeth on him shall*
> *not be ashamed. (Romans 9:30-33)*

God puts people in circumstances where they will either stumble over the stone or recognize it and say, "This is the cornerstone." How can God test us unless He puts a rock of offense in our way? God will create circumstances by which the Church will either be unified or divided.

The first means of separation that God uses to judge us is our lack of hearing by the Holy Spirit. Some people will hear and some will not - but why?

> *[Jesus] answered and said unto*
> *them, Because it is given unto you to*
> *know the mysteries of the kingdom of*
> *heaven, but to them it is not given.*
> *(Matthew 13:11)*

Mysteries are being unfolded today for the Church that have never before been understood. I believe with everything within me that Martin Luther was the man of his day whom God raised up to establish faith in the Church. John Wesley was also a man who put power in the Church. At the turn of the century, the Pentecostal movement brought a new personalization to the Spirit of God and to the Church. The charismatic movement

carried the Spirit of God across lines that people had
drawn and made the Spirit something that belonged to
the total Church, not just to a seemingly select few. Now
we come to another step, and that step is either the
separation or the unity of the Body of Christ at a level
never known before.

> *For whosoever hath, to him shall be
> given, and he shall have more abun-
> dance: but whosoever hath not, from
> him shall be taken away even that he
> hath. Therefore speak I to them in para-
> bles: because **they seeing see not; and
> hearing they hear not, neither do
> they understand.** And in them is ful-
> filled the prophecy of Esaias [Isaiah],
> which saith,*

> *By hearing ye shall hear, and shall
> not understand; and seeing ye shall see,
> and shall not perceive: for this people's
> heart is waxed gross [callous], and their
> ears are dull of hearing, and their eyes
> they have closed; lest at any time they
> should see with their eyes, and hear
> with their ears, and should understand
> with their heart, and should be con-
> verted, and I should heal them. (Mat-
> thew 13:12-15)*

The separated people will not hear because they are
afraid they will be converted and have to change the
path they are traveling. They hear as others hear, but
they will neither give of their savings, nor sacrifice, nor

submit to the hand of God Almighty. Just as Cain, they say, "I have a better way of doing it. I will have my own religion and I will do things the way my mind says to do them." They do not want to be healed because their lifestyles would have to change.

Paul reiterates that the house of Israel is not determined according to heritage or inheritance. He says, "I, too, am of the house of Israel and of the seed of Abraham. But I no longer lay claim to that. For now the election is according to grace. And if it is by grace, then it is no more by works."

David said, "Let their table be made a snare." Many think this has to do with sins and carnalities. The table will now become a snare in which weakness, sickness, and death will move at a proportion never before known in the Body of Christ, as judgment and purification of the Body of Christ.

> *David saith, Let their table be made a snare, and a trap, and a stumblingblock, and a recompence unto them. Let their eyes be darkened that they may not see, and bow down their back alway. I say then, have they stumbled that they should fall? God forbid: but rather through their fall salvation is come unto the Gentiles, to provoke them to jealousy. (Romans 11:9-11)*

No one can separate the Body into separate little groups. National Israel must now understand that spiritual Israel is a vital part of the economy of God. So we see that people are separated first by their lack of hearing and secondly by the table of excuses.

In the gospel according to Luke, there is an account of a great feast (Luke 14:15-24). When all the preparations had been made, the people began to make excuses and to comfort each other with their excuses. The excuse-makers got together in their little groups and said, "We are one."

> *The first said unto him, I have bought a piece of ground, and I must needs go and see it: I pray thee have me excused. And another said, I have bought five yoke of oxen, and I go to prove them: I pray thee have me excused. And another said, I have married a wife, and therefore I cannot come. (Luke 14:18-20)*

The table of the Lord is a constant reminder that in the blood of the Lord is redemption, which brings an ongoing healing to the Body of Christ. Through the drinking of the blood at the table, we obtain forgiveness. The bread is Jesus' body which suggests healing. Isaiah said, "You were healed by His stripes," and Peter said, "You were healed through His body." Not through the **crumbs** of the bread, but through the **body** of Jesus Christ. Jesus said, "This is my body. Take and eat it." In doing so, we bring healing to ourselves, and that is one positive benefit of the table of the Lord.

The second benefit at the Lord's table is the love feast created for the fellowship of saints. The fellowship is not just for the present time; it lasts forever. The marriage supper of the Lamb is a foretaste of what eternity will be like - a constant fellowship with God. The table is the place of fellowship we understand best here on earth. But beyond this finite experience is a fellowship in the Spirit that the table prepares for us.

The third aspect of the Lord's table is one that has not yet been understood properly. As much as the table brings unity, healing, and forgiveness, it is also a table to separate and to purge the people of God. In a spiritual dream, God took me back to the Passover. The primary purpose for the Passover was to separate a people unto God. It was not primarily to bring redemption because the Jews were already God's people by promise. I believe that had there been Egyptians who followed the plan that God had given by sacrificing a lamb and putting its blood on their doorposts because they believed in Jehovah God, the angel of the Lord would have passed over their households just as he passed over the Jewish households. The purpose of the Passover was to find a people of obedience who would do what God said without question, no matter how foolish it seemed to their natural minds. The separation took place at the eating of the Passover. If God is a God of pattern and if He used the table in His early Church as a means of separation, He will still do so today.

At the Last Supper, Jesus said to Judas, "What you do now, do quickly." He did not say, "Leave the table." He said, "Do what you have purposed in your spirit." If you have decided to tear somebody down, to disavow spiritual authority, to speak evil of dignity, to move by the mind of reason, to move by the flesh and not by the spirit - whatever it is, do it. Separation takes place in the heart and in the Spirit at the Lord's table.

The cup of blessing which we bless, is it not the communion of the blood of Christ? The bread which we break, is it

> *not the communion of the body of*
> *Christ? For we being many are one*
> *bread, and one body: for we are par-*
> *takers of that one bread. (I Corinthians*
> *10:16)*

> *Ye cannot drink the cup of the Lord,*
> *and the cup of devils. Ye cannot be*
> *partakers of the Lord's table, and of the*
> *table of devils. (I Corinthians 10:21)*

Unless the Body of Christ comes into unity at the table of God, destruction will result. The Bride can never be found until we learn to commune together at the table of the Lord so that we are one Body and one bread. We cannot drink the cup of the world (fleshly appetites and desires) and the cup of the Lord, too. The two simply cannot coexist.

> *Whether, therefore ye eat, or drink,*
> *or whatsoever ye do, do all to the glory*
> *of God. Give none offence, neither to*
> *the Jews, nor to the Gentiles [Greeks],*
> *nor to the church of God: Even as I*
> *please all men in all things, not seeking*
> *mine own profit, but the profit of many,*
> *that they may be saved. (I Corinthians*
> *10:31-33)*

Paul goes on to point out that Christians have had grave misunderstanding at the table of the Lord.

> *Now in this that I declare unto you I*
> *praise you not, that ye come together*

*not for the better but for the worse. For first of all, when ye come together in the church, I hear that **there are divisions among you**; and I partly believe it. For there must be also heresies among you, that they which are approved may be made manifest among you.*

When ye come together therefore into one place, this is not to eat the Lord's supper. For in eating every one taketh before other his own supper: and one is hungry, and another is drunken. What? have ye not houses to eat and to drink in? or despise ye the church of God, and shame them that have not? What shall I say to you? shall I praise you in this? I praise you not.

For I have received of the Lord that which also I delivered unto you, That the Lord Jesus the same night in which he was betrayed took bread: And when he had given thanks, he brake it, and said, Take, eat: this is my body, which is broken for you: this do in remembrance of me.

After the same manner also he took the cup, when he had supped, saying, This cup is the new testament in my blood: this do ye, as oft as ye drink it, in remembrance of me. For as often as ye eat this bread, and drink this cup, ye do shew the Lord's death till he come.

Wherefore whosoever shall eat this bread, and drink this cup of the Lord, unworthily, shall be guilty of the body and blood of the Lord. But let a man examine himself, and so let him eat of that bread, and drink of that cup. For he that eateth and drinketh unworthily, eateth and drinketh damnation to himself, not discerning the Lord's body. (I Corinthians 11:17-29)

Paul was speaking here to people who did not understand the workings of the Body, of headship, of the fivefold ministry, or of submission and correction. They did not understand because their ears were closed. God is calling today for His Church to have open ears and spirits which fully understand His table in both its unity and its separation.

At the table of judgment the sovereign mind of God is fixed. An individual may become a Pharaoh with a hardened heart, a Judas who is deceived, or one who is sifted of Satan, but those whose spirits are right will be able to sit at the Lord's table and receive all the healing, forgiveness, and unity that God desires to offer them.

How is the Kingdom of God associated with the table of the Lord? I would reiterate that God's purpose for putting man upon the earth was to correct a situation that had gone wrong. God gave man dominion over the earth and fellowshipped with him on an intimate level, and the Church must reestablish once again that same order and relationship with God. God must find a Body that can be a witness to the world to such a degree that

God will be justified in bringing judgment to the world.

The harvest is much nearer than we realize, and the firstfruit of the harvest - separation - will take place at the table of the Lord. God allows the wheat and the tares to grow along together because He knows that the time of separation will eventually come at the table of the Lord. The tares will be separated by their murmuring and complaining spirits, for sooner or later, out of the abundance of the heart, the mouth will speak.

We must judge ourselves at the table of the Lord, and we must judge no one else. After we have judged ourselves, if we find ourselves lacking, there is still time for repentance and a change of heart before we leave the table.

Then with right spirits, we may continue in the things of God and begin to call to our bridegroom. One day every knee shall bow and every tongue shall confess that Jesus Christ is King of kings and Lord of lords. The Church will be His Bride, and He will be our King. Then shall the earth know that the fullness of God has come.

CHAPTER FIVE
THE GLORIFIED CHURCH

I believe the Lord gave me the spiritual dream I have described to reiterate that the Body of Christ has been wounded, and as long as it is in its wounded state, it cannot do the work of God authoritatively on the earth to the extent that will be necessary to accomplish God's purposes. Our ultimate goal, therefore, must be to establish a Church that is glorified and approved by God. Until the Church reaches that place, it cannot be the incarnation or the full manifestation of God's power on the earth. Jesus correctly declared, "All authority is given me in heaven and in earth," but He also said, without any apology, "Now I transfer that authority to you to such a degree that the things I have done, you shall do in greater measure because I go to my Father."

Was Jesus speaking mere words, or was He proclaiming a great truth that we have overlooked? If we believe His statement to be a great truth, we must also admit that it is not, in fact, the actual case. The Church has known breakthroughs here and there by the Spirit of God, but **as a whole**, we have not acted with the authority that Jesus gave us.

WHAT IS THE GLORIFIED CHURCH?

The glorified Church is a gifted Church. When Jesus came forth from hell, the Word declares that He gave gifts unto men, "some, apostles; and some, prophets; and some, evangelists; and some, pastors and teachers" (Ephesians 4:11). All five of these ministries will be present and active in the glorified Church.

Jesus also gave to the Church the gifts of the Spirit.

All of the gifts of the Spirit will be present in the glorified Church. The glorified Church must be a discerning Church. Hebrews 5:14 speaks of exercising the spiritual gifts so that we might be able to discern, and this is an absolute necessity in these last days when deception can be so subtle that even the very elect can be deceived. Deception is recognized and dealt with only by discernment.

HOW DOES THE GLORIFIED CHRIST DIFFER FROM JESUS OF NAZARETH?

As the glorified Christ, Jesus is no longer restricted by natural laws. He is no longer confined, as such, to an earthly tabernacle or a natural body. As the glorified Christ, He could move through walls without opening doors, and He was able to ascend into heaven as the disciples watched Him because He was no longer constrained by the natural law of gravity. As the glorified Christ, Jesus' greatest desire was to transfer His authority to the Church. All that He had been, He has asked us to become.

By the Spirit of God, I submitted earlier that the seventeenth chapter of John was the prayer that Jesus prayed at His Father's throne after He had ascended into heaven, for He prayed the prayer in the past tense, as though the events He spoke of had already taken place. In His prayer, Jesus prayed that the Church might be unified and also that it might return to its great glory.

In that prayer, Jesus also said, "I pray not that thou shouldest take them out of the world, but that thou shouldest keep them from the evil" (John 17:15). That statement is quite contrary to many of the concepts we have heard across the last few years which have held that the Church will be raptured out of this world. The glorified Church must touch the world to such an extent that the world will believe that the Church is divine, but the Church cannot have that impact if it is raptured or taken out of the world. The problem today is that the world does not believe that the Church is divinely appointed or ordained. They see it as just another institution. When the Church reaches the state of its glorification, it will be far more than just another institution.

> And the glory which thou gavest me I have given them; that they may be one, even as we are one: I in them, and thou in me, that they may be made perfect in one; and that the world may know that thou has sent me, and hast loved them, as thou hast loved me. Father, I will that they also, whom thou hast given me, be with me where I am; that they may behold my glory, which thou hast given me: for thou lovedst me before the foundation of the world. (John 17:22-24)

As the Church achieves the unity for which Jesus was pleading, it will have the authority to stand fast in the face of great tribulation in these last days.

> Herein is our love made perfect, that we may have boldness in the day of judgment: because as he is, so are we in this world. (I John 4:17)

The goal of the incarnate Church must be to become

the incarnate Christ in the world, to become the glorified Church as Jesus was the glorified Christ.

The glorified Church will then be the Bride, able to bring Jesus Christ back to earth as the bridegroom. We are begotten of God, even as Jesus Himself was begotten of God. He was the firstfruit, the elder brother, but we are also the begotten of God as He was. He was the incarnate of God in the past and will be the incarnate of God in the future for eternity, but we, the Church, are now His Body and the only Christ in the world today. At this point, there is no other incarnation of God in the world, and for that reason we must set our affections on things above and be about God's business.

The glorified Church will bring the return of the glorified Christ. There cannot be a union until we are prepared to live in the fullness of Christ. We are now in the midst of that preparation. We are already the temple of God; we are that house not made with hands. In Isaiah 62:12 we are called a "sought out people." In I Peter 2:9-10 we are called "a chosen generation, a royal priesthood, a peculiar people." These are all various names given to one group of people - the Bride of Christ.

In the fourth chapter of the Song of Solomon, there is a description of the beautiful woman who is the Bride of Christ - the glorified Church. The beautiful, mature Bride is no longer like the little girl who is not fully developed or the little girl who cannot discern. She is now a woman who is physically and mentally prepared to be the Bride of Christ.

In the Revelation, John saw the Bride, and from his writings we learn who she is.

John said, And there came unto me

> *one of the seven angels who had the
> seven bowls full of the seven last
> plagues, and talked with me, saying,
> Come hither, I will shew thee the bride,
> the Lamb's wife. And he carried me
> away in the spirit to a great and a high
> mountain, and shewed me that great
> city, the holy Jerusalem, descending
> out of heaven from God, Having the
> glory of God: and her light was like unto
> a stone most precious, even like a jasper
> stone, clear as crystal. (Revelation
> 21:9-10)*

The glory and anointing of God come down from
God out of heaven and reside in the new Jerusalem,
which represents the people of God. The Bride is the
people of God. I have heard some blessed brethren
preach lately that the new Jerusalem is a planet orbiting
the earth, spinning around in the heavens somewhere
waiting to descend to the earth. The Word of God
contains neither pattern to prove this theory nor scriptures to concur with it. The glory, the gifts and every
other good thing that comes from God comes down
from Him out of heaven, and His glory descends upon
His Church, His people - the New Jerusalem.

WHERE IS CHRIST?

Jesus is waiting in the heavens until the earth has
been restored by the Church of the Living God. The
bridegroom cannot come again until the Bride has
finished her preparation, and before Jesus can return to
the earth, the Church must be glorified.

God does not predetermine people; He predeter-
mines plans. We have been foreordained of God to
become that people of God who will be so glorified that
we can bring Christ back to the earth. This glorified
Church must make the earth God's footstool before
Jesus can come again.

> But this man, after he had offered
> one sacrifice for sins for ever, sat down
> on the right hand of God; From hence-
> forth expecting till his enemies be made
> His footstool. (Hebrews 10:12-13)

WHY DOES THE BRIDEGROOM WAIT?

There is a scripture in John 14 which I have personally used many times at funerals, but which is usually
used totally out of context. Jesus said,

> Let not your heart be troubled: ye
> believe in God, believe also in me. In
> my Father's house are many mansions:
> if it were not so, I would have told you. I
> go to prepare a place for you. And if I go
> and prepare a place for you, I will come
> again, and receive you unto myself; that
> where I am, there ye may be also. (John
> 14:1-3)

Jesus is saying, "I am going to prepare a place where
we can dwell together." No scripture is of private inter-
pretation, neither can it be taken out of context. The
context for this scripture is, "I am going to go away to a

place where I will stay while the Church grows up and becomes the habitation of God. I will send you another Comforter, the Holy Spirit, who will prepare the people of God to become My Bride. Then I will come again and we will dwell together."

WHERE ARE THE DEAD IN CHRIST TODAY?

The bodies of the dead in Christ are in the ground, and their spirits are being reserved wherever Christ is. We do not know where the souls of the saints are, but we do know where their bodies are. We also know that Christ is going to bring them with Him when He returns and put their spirits back into them. Those who are alive when Christ returns will not be more important than those who have died, because those who have died in Christ will rise first. Then we who are alive will be "caught up."

Those words - "caught up" - have been interpreted in many different ways. When we see the bridegroom coming, we will be so excited about it that we will be caught up with glory. We will be caught up in the clouds, which always represent the presence and the glory of God. Being "caught up" does not necessarily mean we will leave the earth and ascend to heaven as Christ did.

This theory of the "catching up" or "catching away" can be devastating to the maturing Body of Christ. Poor old saints are just sitting around waiting to die or to be raptured, never maturing, never growing up, never putting their foot on the head of the serpent, never saying, "I am made to be a son of God." Instead of waiting to be caught up, they ought to be saying, "I'm going to **grow up** and not **go up** so the Church can become the mature Bride of Christ."

This is the mystery of the Kingdom. "We shall not all sleep [die], but we shall all be changed" (I Corinthians 15:51). This is the glorified Church who will finally reach the place where she will be changed. Enoch was the firstfruit example of this concept.

What quality enabled Enoch to bypass death and go directly home to be with God? Hebrews 11:5 tells us, "...before his translation he had this testimony, that **he pleased God** ." We know from the verse that follows (11:6) that "without faith it is **impossible** to please him." We **cannot** please God without faith. Therefore, the Church that is seasoned in faith will please God. The Church that overcomes by faith will not die. At the last trumpet, the dead will be raised and the glorified Church shall be changed.

Let me describe the glorified Church. **The glorified Church will be approved by the Father.** The glorified Church that we are looking for may not be made up of a great number of people. It may be only a nucleus of people, a firstfruit, but somewhere on the face of this earth, there will be a people - numerically how large or small I do not know - whose number will be adequate to become a witness of God to the nations of the earth.

The glorified Church will be a mature Church. It will be a Church that is no longer splintered. As Paul describes in Ephesians 4, it will be a Church unified in **faith** - not in doctrine, mode, practice, or organization - but by the Spirit of unity in Christ. Organizations cannot bring about the glorified Church through ecumenical movements. I believe the Holy Spirit will bring together people from around the earth whom the Spirit of God will unite to become the Bride of Christ, mature and able to transcend doctrinal or organizational differences.

The glorified, mature Bride will be well-mannered.
A mature Body of believers does not have to be told the
same things over and over again. The mature Bride of
Christ doesn't have to be told to use a fork when she
should be using a spoon. She has graduated from the
finishing school of faith and is polished and mature.

The mature Church is also confident. One of the
most beautiful things in the world is a young woman
who has reached a place of confidence and knows how
to hold her head up high and walk tall. Likewise, the
mature Bride is confident because she knows who she
is. She knows how to love unconditionally. She does not
love only to receive love in return. She loves others in
spite of their inability to love her back.

**The mature Bride has put away childish things
and is now complete in her faith.** She knows the
difference between crying in intercession before the
Lord and begging God for things all the time. An imma-
ture Bride is always begging, but never seeks after what
is good for the household. She is not like the virtuous
woman described in Proverbs 31, who knows how to
use her talents and how to move in faith.

The mature Bride knows she is somebody. She can
stand up in the face of the devil when everything seems
to be falling apart. Her faith will take her through the
wilderness, through rivers, and even through death
without failing because the Bride has learned that faith is
something the mature Body of Christ must have.

The glorified Church is empowered. Jesus said,
"The things that I do, ye shall do, and **greater** because I
go to the Father." Jesus said He would empower us with
such authority that even the gates of hell could not stop
us. No less than the authority of hell will have to be
subservient to us! The glorified Church will know that

she has the authority and power to storm the very gates of hell itself.

The glorified Church has the power to loose and to bind. Whatever she looses on this earth will be loosed in heaven. Whatever she binds on this earth will be bound in heaven. Only the mature Body of Christ will be trusted to such a degree that God will not transcend her authority. He will recognize whatever we loose or whatever we bind on earth. The glorified Church will speak with authority, and she will know how to pray a mature prayer. God must be able to trust His Church on the earth because as the Bride of Christ, she is the literal expression of God and His power and love made manifest to the world.

HOW WILL THE GLORIFIED CHURCH APPEAR?

Let us look first of all at Jesus Christ the Incarnate. Born in due season in God's own time, He came forth from the womb of the virgin Mary, who had conceived of the Holy Spirit. We see that incarnate Christ in the gospels, but we see a different Christ in John's Revelation. There we see a glorified Christ. The first chapter of the Revelation, beginning in verse twelve, gives us an idea of the differences between the incarnate and the glorified Christ.

> *And I [John] turned to see the voice that spake with me. And being turned, I saw seven golden candlesticks; And in the midst of the seven candlesticks one like unto the Son of man, clothed with a garment down to the foot [symbolizing His judgment as the judge of eternity],*

*and girt about the paps [breast] with a
golden girdle [royalty].*

*His head and his hairs were white like
wool, as white as snow [wisdom,
omniscience]; and his eyes were as a
flame of fire [discernment]; And his feet
like unto fine brass, as if they burned in
a furnace [ability to move in the anointing, as well as the glory He had known
with His Father before the incarnation];
and his voice as the sound of many
waters.*

*And he had in his right hand seven
stars: and out of his mouth went a sharp,
two-edged sword: and his countenance
was as the sun shineth in his strength.*

*And when I saw him, I fell at his feet
as dead. And he laid his right hand
upon me, saying unto me, Fear not; I
am the first and last: I am he that liveth,
and was dead; and, behold, I am alive
for evermore, Amen; and have the keys
of hell and of death. (Revelation
1:12-18)*

There is quite a difference in the incarnate Christ
described in the gospels and the glorified Christ pictured
in John's Revelation. In the garden Jesus said to Mary,
"Don't touch me yet, for I've not yet gone back to My
Father." But after He had gone to the Father for the
approval of His sacrifice, He returned as the glorified
Christ.

The glorified Church is a willing Church. God cannot work with anyone who is not willing, and He greatly desires that our wills be set to follow Him. Because the glorified Church is a willing Church, we must be willing to give and to work.

I believe in the not-too-distant future, the glorious day will come when the Holy Spirit of God will tell the Bride, who is the Church, that it is now time for the bridegroom to come. The Church is beginning to approach that place of glorification where in her Spirit she, too, knows that the hour is drawing closer. She is preparing herself and making all things ready. She is filling her hope chest. When she has completed the finishing school of faith, she can begin to look up and say with the authority born of maturity, "Come, Lord Jesus, come."

When the trumpet shall sound, we who remain shall be changed gloriously in the twinkling of an eye, and the King of kings and the Lord of lords shall descend in glory out of the heavens. He will bid His Bride to come and sit beside Him to rule and reign with Him on this earth that has once again been made His footstool.

We are now approaching that hour. The Bride is being prepared. Nations are being turned around by the authority of the Church, and this is God's hour for the glorified Church to come forth, mature and without spot or wrinkle, to be approved of God.

CHAPTER SIX
QUESTIONS AND DISCUSSION

After I completed this series of messages on the wounded Body of Christ, I gave the members of the congregation an opportunity to ask questions about any of the topics I had covered. I have chosen the questions which were most representative of those that were asked, and hopefully they will answer any questions which you may have had in your mind. The answers have been recorded just as they were given.

Is there a difference between the glorious Church and the glorified Church?

Since we have heard both terms used, there may be some confusion about them. I personally do not believe the two should be used interchangeably.

For many years, we have sung songs about the "glorious Church, without spot or wrinkle, washed in the blood of the Lamb." I believe that we, today, are glorious people of God, just as the early Christians who were imprisoned for their beliefs were also glorious people of God.

But I consider the glorified Church to be mature and more able to share communion with the glorified Christ. It is the Church that God has approved because her work has been well done, a Church to whom God can say, "You have accomplished your task and now you may enter into the joy of the Lord."

So I would say that when we are speaking of the Church that is ready to meet the bridegroom, the term we use should be "glorified Church," as opposed to "glorious Church."

In relation to your preaching about the Spirit of truth and fact, please explain and give examples of the two.

It was a **truth** that Jesus said He was a king, but that **fact** was part of putting Him on the cross. Now the greater **truth** was that He was the King whom God had sent, but **fact** had the people believing that He wanted to unseat the political leaders of Jerusalem, Judea, Palestine, and perhaps eventually even Rome. **Fact** caused people to consider Jesus a threat to civil authority, but that was never His approach or attitude at all.

Now let me illustrate the spirit of truth. Jesus was sent to become the King who would restore the earth. One of the great problems I find with our laws in the United States is that sometimes we seem to be more concerned with fact than we are with the spirit of truth. The **fact** is that we may not stop dead still at a stop sign thirty miles out in the country where there is no traffic, but the **spirit** of the fact is that if our car rolls through the stop sign, there is still total safety. Some police officers will stop people in deserted places for allowing their cars to roll instead of coming to a complete stop, and many people become rebellious against the police because they fail to understand that the spirit of the law is safety and protection.

The **fact** was that Noah was drunk, but the spirit of **truth** said that because he was a man God had used, more than his flesh needed to be considered at that moment. Fact can become a very strong weapon in the hands of Satan, but the spirit of truth always sets free.

You may say, "Well, it ought to be black or white. It ought to be one way or the other." But it cannot be that way. Some may say that in the world, a question can always be answered "yes" or "no," but that is not true. Let me give you one question that cannot be answered without incrimination. After I give the question, answer it mentally. The question is, "Men, have you stopped beating your wife?"

If you answer yes, you have just admitted that you have indeed been beating your wife. If you say no, then you are admitting that you're **still** beating your wife. So it should be quite evident by now that "yes" and "no" are not always as clear-cut as they seem. It is the **spirit** of truth that sets free.

Must there be a total unity of faith with all believers before the Lord comes back? Just how close is the Kingdom of God to being fully established or manifested?

I do not believe that we can answer numerically how broadly this truth must be accepted in the Church universal, but I would say that there must come such a spirit of unity that it is known worldwide. Remember that Jesus said, "And this gospel of the kingdom shall be preached in all the world for a witness unto all nations" (Matthew 24:14). Although the gospel of the Kingdom is a gospel of unity, that does not mean that every little fragmented part of what we term "Christian people" must stand in total unity of faith. It **does** mean that the Church will be matured and unified to the point where the world will feel the **impact** of its unity. It will no longer present a fragmented, splintered appearance to the world.

There must be a true oneness, not a mere unity of doctrine. There can never and will never be a unity of doctrine. I don't believe Jesus had that even among His disciples. But what He did have - and what we must strive for - is a spirit of unity of faith that says that Jesus Christ is Lord and that He answers all the needs of mankind.

So I cannot quote specific numbers, but I believe there will have to be a worldwide impact of our unity. We cannot have unity so long as the church is seen as a Grecian branch, a Roman branch, a Pentecostal branch, or an Evangelical branch. We must achieve such unity in the eyes of the world that people can say, "**This** is the Body of Christ."

How close are we to achieving that unity? If you and I diligently did the work that God called us to do, I believe it would be frightening how close we really are. I believe the demonstration of the Kingdom in the spirit of unity is very, very close because people around the world are growing hungry to see the Body of Christ unified. I believe the Kingdom could very well be manifested within the lifespan of the generation that has just been born.

We spoke of the healing of the wounded Body of Christ, yet you said that some have been separated at the table of the Lord. Please explain how separation can be healing to the Body. This seems like a contradiction.

If there were a foreign object in your body, it would have to be removed before the sore could heal. If you had a thorn in your foot, you wouldn't have to cast out a devil. You would just pull the thorn out. Sometimes before there can be unity, there must be separation. The spirit of Delilah and the spirit of Christ cannot sit at the same table. But we cannot bring that separation. Jesus made that point clear because He said that were we to do the separating, we might separate good people. For that reason, only God can bring separation. He allows people to go on until their fruit becomes so obvious that they separate themselves.

So it is not a contradiction. The table of the Lord that brings unity must also bring separation both in us and from those who divide the Body of Christ (Romans 16: 17-18).

Sometimes before people can get well, they must be separated because God didn't join them together in the first place. Some people may say, "We were sinners when we got married, so we ought to get a divorce now." No, that's a cop-out. If both were saved and were ever unified in Christ, then Christ made them one in Him, and what they need to do is straighten up their act and solve their problems.

But if there is actually such a strong difference where one is following the ways of the world and Satan while the other is going the way of God, then sometimes before healing can come into a family, there must be a separation. Sometimes before a young person can be healed, he must be removed from a group of his peers who are causing him to go astray.

So separation bringing healing is not a contradiction. It is simply a matter of bringing together those whom God has joined together.

The next question is perhaps a follow-up to the one I just addressed.

Will you please relate the role of the Covenant Kingdom Communities in our Church to the process of healing the wounded Body and bringing forth the glorified Church?

I literally believe the words of the Apostle Paul when he said, "Rejoice with them that do rejoice, and weep with them that weep" (Romans 12:15). I believe there is healing in the love of Christ and virtue in the Body of the Church just as there was virtue in the physical body of Christ. For that reason I believe there must be a closeness between us in our covenant communities. I know there are risks involved when spiritual people are put together in social situations because there is always a chance of surfacing the flesh, but even at that risk, it is God's only method of bringing us into a relationship so we can minister to one another.

This may raise questions from people who don't know our total ministry. But sometimes homes fall apart because a married couple so totally keeps to itself that they never broaden the base of their relationship. Eventually they become so isolated that after awhile, their relationship sours and dies. They may live under the same roof, but they have no life because they have not broadened their relationship in the family of Christ. Many people should feed our lives, and likewise we should feed the lives of others. That helps to keep us in balance.

For example, my wife Norma cannot perform every function that I need in my life. There was a time when she was the church pianist, she was a mother - in short, she served many functions in my life and in the life of the church. Now, though, I must have secretaries, children's directors, and pastors, among other things, because it would wear Norma out if she tried to do everything. Out of necessity, we had to broaden the base of those who were involved in our ministry. If I had tried to keep Norma doing all those things out of possessiveness, I would have been in error. And if she had tried to hang onto me out of possessiveness, then she would not have understood the covenant community relationship either.

The covenant community is God's way of actually bringing the concept of God in the flesh into reality. And yes, I do believe the covenant communities will help bring about the unity of faith.

How do we cross doctrinal boundaries to fellowship with other members of the Body who deny our beliefs, such as the baptism of the Holy Spirit or speaking in tongues?

I believe some people do not really deny the baptism of the Holy Spirit; they simply don't understand it. If they don't understand it, then I believe our fellowship should be open and free with them. But if they call the Holy Ghost the work of the devil, that is a lie from which we must back off, because such a statement is not of God and will only bring destruction.

If they simply have not been enlightened, they may say, "I have not received the baptism with the evidence of speaking with other tongues, but since it was used in the early church, maybe God can still use it today." I have no problem with that. We can fellowship with those who preach a strong doctrine of Jesus Christ, even though they may never have received the baptism as we know it. But if they begin to say the baptism is of the devil, it becomes blasphemous and that is where the line must be drawn.

We cannot compromise what we know to be true just to create fellowship, because fellowship must be within areas that God approves. Sometimes these may be areas in which people have misunderstandings or differences, but as long as their spirits remain right with God, fellowship is possible and may yield beneficial results to everyone involved.

We are living in the period when the scriptures say that if it were possible, the very elect would be deceived. Knowing that the Spirit of the antichrist is so prevalent in our very midst and having such a high calling for discernment of the counterfeit, what words of caution and/or exhortation can you give so that we will have the confidence we need in a time such as this and so we won't be deceived?

First of all, in terms of the local church, I put down a stake in the authority of God's Word which is divine, sovereign authority. Next, Chapel Hill Harvester Church is an open ministry where other pastors come in and prophesy among us and judge us. We also have national pastors' conferences which are open to hundreds of pastors who can review any aspect of our ministry, right down to our financial records. Another criterion is, "Wherefore by their fruits ye shall know them" (Matthew 7:20). What is the fruit of a ministry? Is it creating love? Is it setting people free from bondage? Is it lifting up Christ? These are criteria by which we know that we will not be deceived.

Deception usually hides itself. It cloaks and masks itself. Deception was personified in Jim Jones who took people off to an island, segregated them from the world, and started drugging their minds and tearing up the Bible. Jim Jones said, "I'm the authority," and literally took the Bible, threw it to the ground, and stomped on it. Obviously, if we were in a situation like that, we would know we were in deception. So there are ways and means which will keep us from being deceived. The spirit of truth will always set us free and bring us many evidences that keep us from deception.

Another criterion which gives us confidence about the credence of a local ministry is that it is never afraid to be judged, not by the world but by the Church itself. Not long ago I received a letter from Dean David Collins, one of the great spiritual leaders of the world, who now heads the largest Episcopal church in the United States. In that letter he suggested that I represented charismatics and Pentecostals to the world, and to me that represents approval from a high authority. When Bishop Benson Idahosa of Nigeria, or Bishop Robert McAlister of Brazil or Iverna Tompkins says that Chapel Hill Harvester Church is a sovereign move of Almighty God, then we are not building ourselves up. When the voice of another confirms what God is doing, that gives protection and safety.

As the glorified Church, what does it mean to rule and reign with Christ? Where will that rule and reign exist?

The first area in which we learn to rule and reign is in our own lives by learning temperance and control of our spirits and tongues - in short, by learning how to control ourselves. Then we learn to rule and reign in a social setting, that is, as we relate to others in the Body of Christ. Then, as we learn to deal with spirits, we begin to move into higher areas of ruling and reigning with Christ because the Bible tells us that we wrestle not against flesh and blood but against principalities and powers (Ephesians 6:12). Next we begin to take dominion in spiritual areas by casting out devils and by discerning spirits rather than just personalities. Finally we begin to rule and reign with Christ.

We rule and reign, then, internally, in a social setting; in the heavenlies; and finally here upon the earth when we will rule and reign in a setting like that which Adam and Eve knew with God in the Garden of Eden. I would add to this, however, my personal belief which I speak as Paul did, "by permission" (I Corinthians 7:6). From the evidence of the nature of the resurrected Body of Christ, I believe that we will not only rule and reign but that this earth will be the home base of the glorified Church and the fellowship of Christ. This is where the New Jerusalem - the Bride - will remain.

I also believe that we will have access to more of the universe and to the creative processes of God. Jesus was able to ascend to His Father and if He was able to do so, then I have no reason to assume that we might not have some of the same capabilities and rights. But that's not really something I would want to try to prove at this point. The basic place where we will rule and reign is on the earth. There is not one scripture that suggests we'll ever rule and reign with Christ anywhere but here on the earth.

If brothers or sisters in Christ do not embrace the revelation we have been given, what should be our attitude and/or response toward them?

The first response should be to give them what truth you think they can handle, as the Lord leads. If you try to attack them immediately in some of their very sacred doctrines, you're going to be in difficulty. First of all, love them because love can transcend any differences that may exist. Then if you believe they are in error, give them an opportunity to learn by giving them pamphlets or other written materials. Most of all, though, just give them love.

A proper attitude is one which lets them know that you yourself were at one time just where they are, and in certain areas of revelation you may still be where they are. Who knows how much revelation yet remains and how many mysteries have not yet been unfolded? Deuteronomy 29:29 says, "The secret things belong unto the Lord our God: but those things which are revealed belong unto us..." God has not given all of His revelation, and there are still many things we don't know. But the one thing we do know is that when God has given us a positive revelation, we can stand pat.

God has given me certain revelations that I would die for because I **know** they are of God. I know there are certain doctrines, still being strictly adhered to, which are but detours that we get off on sometimes. But I believe we need to hold to the greater truths to bring about the unity of faith instead of the unity of doctrine.

A proper attitude should be one of love and openness. Our response should not be one of defensiveness because if we have truth, we don't need to be defensive.

We can sit back and relax and say, "I'm going to love you, and would you just read this literature and give God a little time?"

I constantly receive letters and telephone calls from pastors who tell me, "God also spoke to me concerning the things I've heard you preach, but I was afraid to preach them myself." A pastor wrote to me and said, "When I started preaching these things a year or so ago, my church was dying. To date we have added over five hundred new members in the last six months." The same thing is happening all across the nation because people don't want to just sit around and wait to die; they want an army to be built and they want to be part of a sovereign move of God. The secrets of growth do not lie in how large a staff a church has or whether a church has an elaborate computer system or how great the choir is. **Growth comes when a church has the message of God that the world is hungry and thirsty to hear.** When that message is preached, the world will come to hear it and the church will grow, no matter what else it has to offer.

Must the whole Church be made up of true believers who reach the full stature of Christ in order for Him to return, or is there a number that would be sufficient to bring about this glorified state?

First I will talk about the local church and then about the Church universal. In the local church there will never be a time when we can identify, per se, who is part of the glorified Church and who is not because that is the work of the Holy Spirit. When people desire to join the church, we receive them on the evidence of their word and their testimony. We don't know how many people in a core group must be enlightened before God can use a church as a great prophetic or healing church. Neither can I say how many in the world must become subservient to a vision God has given.

I do believe, however, that an enlightened church must have a world impact in order to counter the spirit of the antichrist which also has a world impact. In some ways, the spirit of the antichrist has a more powerful impact than the Church of Jesus Christ because the authorities of earthly governments are still ruled, for the most part, by powers and principalities.

In light of that, we must understand that the Church must gain such unity of faith that it will have a profound impact on the world. The Church must speak so that the whole world will listen, and that just isn't true now. When the Pope speaks, Catholics listen in the parts of the world where Catholics are predominant, but before Christ can come again, the time will come when the Church must take such a strong a stand that the whole world will say, "That is the voice of God speaking to us."

How many will it take? Five thousand? Five million? Five hundred million? I don't know, but God will soon look down and say, "That number is sufficient for a witness."

God told Satan to look at Job, and Job, who represents the contest between God and Satan, symbolizes the Church. The Church today is in that same contest and the Church must prove that it will not deny God, even as Job had to do. "Though he [God] slay me, yet will I trust in him " (Job 13:15). When Job stood up and dusted himself off and claimed to be the son of God, he received deliverance and God was able to say, "See, Satan, I told you he wouldn't fail."

The last enemy to be conquered is death and who will conquer it? A mature church will come forth with the kind of authority and power that will be able to stand in the very face of Satan. When the Church reaches that state of maturity, God will be able to say, "There is no need for the Church to die. She has reached a place of maturity, and because that pleases me, I will translate her." What was the testimony about Enoch? **He pleased God.** When the Church becomes so mature that as a Body we have achieved the unity of faith, God will find her pleasing and say, "She is mature enough now, and she doesn't have to die."

Did I understand you to say that those influenced by the Spirit of the antichrist believe that Christ came in the flesh but do not believe that Christ is made manifest through the Church? Would you elaborate on this?

When John dealt with this issue, he said the spirit of the antichrist was already at work and was identifiable by the fact that it "...confesseth not that Jesus Christ is come in the flesh..." (I John 4:3). It is in this area that we must test the spirits.

The greatest test of the spirit of the antichrist is its attitude toward the church. The attitude isn't directed toward Jesus because Jesus is not personally a threat to any community unless there is a living, thriving church functioning in that community. The spirit of the antichrist, therefore, will not recognize that God is here in the flesh.

Consider some of the popular entertainers who make fun of the church today and study their lives. They do not attack Jesus Christ, nor do they talk about Jesus who lived in Jerusalem off the shores of Galilee. Instead they attack Oral Roberts and Kenneth Copeland and Jim Bakker. They attack the Church of Jesus Christ and its representatives because that is the area in which the spirit of the antichrist operates most successfully.

"Even now **already** it is in the world" (I John 4:3). Many people are waiting for one man to appear who has the ability to put the number 666 on us, never knowing that because six is one short of seven (perfection), six is the number of man himself. The number of man has always existed and by discernment it can be identified today.

We know that the mark will be found in man's forehead - his mind and thought patterns - and in his hand - his work patterns. We get into difficulty because we try to identify **literally** concepts that John was describing symbolically because he was living in a day and age of great persecution. His words meant nothing to a carnal Roman Empire, but they symbolized concepts he was trying to convey to the Christians to whom he was writing. He used numbers because they were always significant to the Jewish people: twelve tribes of Israel, twelve apostles, seven churches. It is vital that we be in touch with the spirit beyond the revelation because it is still significant for us today.

Can the Bride of Christ develop in another part of the world and we here in the United States not be aware of it and therefore have the coming of the Bridegroom take us by surprise?

Jesus warned, "Don't let that day overtake you as a

thief in the night." I personally will not let that happen to me. I'm going to keep my eyes and ears open and if I see or hear of a mature Bride in Australia which I know is a witness to the world and doing things for God, I'll say, "Praise God, that is a part of the Bride of Christ."

I do believe that the Bride can begin to mature in different parts of the world, but she will still have to have a world-wide impact. When that happens, we will be aware that the Church of Jesus Christ is making that impact.

That is already happening today in some parts of the world. When we were in Nigeria, we were told by that country's highest authority that Benson Idahosa and his church have single-handedly changed Nigeria's existing laws about witches and witchcraft, and that is certainly a witness to the nations of the earth. This is but one evidence that the Bride is growing up and beginning to let the world know who she is.

Will you further explain loosing and binding on earth and in Heaven?

The terms, loosing and binding, frighten people, but the Church has the authority to send people to heaven or hell. Let me explain that. Perhaps there is a man living in a hovel in South America who is lost because he has never heard the name of Jesus Christ. If a missionary goes into that country, taking the keys of the Kingdom, and tells that man about Jesus, the missionary's authority is the same authority that Peter had when he dealt with Ananias and Sapphira.

Peter said, "Ananias, why hath Satan filled thine heart to lie to the Holy Ghost?...thou hast not lied unto men, but unto God" (Acts 5:3-4). When Ananias heard Peter's words, he fell down dead. When Peter later confronted Sapphira with the same accusation, she lied as Ananias had done, and Peter said, "The feet of them which have buried thy husband are at the door, and shall carry thee out" (Acts 5:9). And she, too, fell to the ground dead. Peter actually had the authority to tell Ananias and Sapphira to drop dead.

Is that a frightening thought? God is going to have such trust in the mature Church that He will give her the authority to loose and bind. We have not reached that place yet, but I have seen the firstfruits of it. Things are taking place in different areas of the world, and even in Atlanta, that cause us to know this is true.

God will also give His Church the authority to loose and bind in terms of loosing people with the knowledge that Jesus Christ is Lord. That was really the confession which brought about the deaths of Ananias and Sapphira. It was not the person of Peter that caused their deaths - it was Peter's confession that Jesus was the Christ. We, as the Church, have the keys to loose and bind and, in some cases, the keys even to curse and to bless, but that will come only when the Church is mature enough to handle that authority.

Will the Lord raise up prophetic churches in all localities? What do people do who hear and recognize truth through our outreach ministry but become frustrated because they cannot find the same teachings in their local churches?

This is one of the issues we deal with most often in the mail we receive. We get letters from people who are

ready to give up what we call the "charismatic experience" because of the shallowness of the churches in
their area.

One of the marvels of our day is that we have evidences that make us know that Jesus could come in the
lifetime of this generation, while in other generations
this could not have been true. For example, Peter said,
"The heavens shall pass away with a great noise, and
the elements shall melt with fervent heat, the earth also
and the works that are therein shall be burned up" (II
Peter 3:10). This was not so in other generations
because no generation until ours has had the nuclear
bombs which are capable of causing the destruction that
Peter described. Revelation 1:7 says that when Christ
comes again, "every eye shall see him," and that could
never have been true before this age of television and
advanced telecommunications. All things are coming to
a peak in our generation.

What we must understand is that we are on the very
threshold. If we could only know that the cares of this
life, the frustrations, and even mental depressions are
just obstacles to be overcome. God wants us to have
sound minds. He does not want us to go around looking
like a dog that has just been whipped! We will never
bring in the Kingdom of God if we walk around looking
like we just lost our last friend! We have to perk up and
say, "I don't care how the devil attacks me because I
know who wrote the last line, and we're going to win this
battle!" I believe that if we truly believed that we just
might be the ones to bring Jesus Christ back, we would
so seek first the Kingdom of God that everything else
would fall in line. When it seems that we are getting
bogged down in unimportant areas, I just say, "Devil,
you might have won this round, but I've got news for

you - you haven't won the battle yet. We're going to get you in the last round, because we're going to bring Jesus Christ back to this earth!"

The Bible says that in the new age, we will not marry or be given in marriage. Should we remain single now to prepare for that?

If you want to miss the joys of life now, you can, but I wouldn't! I'm not sure we would know how to be related in a Kingdom relationship if we didn't know how to be related in an earthly relationship now. Everything we do now must be on a limited basis because God cannot trust mankind. God didn't say that He made Adam and Eve husband and wife; He said that He made them male and female. Nothing was said about marriage in the Garden. That was something that came about later.

Jesus put it in perspective when He said, "In the kingdom they neither marry, nor are given in marriage" (Mark 12:25). When we come to that place, we will be like the angels because God will be able to trust us. Anyone who thinks that it will be one big orgy simply doesn't understand that sex as we know it does not touch what God has in store for us.

People have become so preoccupied with sex that some of them have even said, "I don't want to go to heaven if we won't have sex." They just don't understand God. If God could make an apple, think of what He could do if He really tried. If He put just a little effort into it, He could do things we've never even thought of. So we should not spend our time worrying about what is going to happen in the new age. We should be learning how to maintain and live in good relationships now. How will God be able to trust us in Kingdom relationships in heaven if He can't trust us in earthly relationships now?

Matthew 24:35 says, "Heaven and earth shall pass away, but my words shall not pass away." If Heaven and earth do indeed pass away, where will the glorified Church be in the new age?

Heaven and earth, as we know them, shall pass away because as Peter said, "The earth shall be purged by fire" (II Peter 3:10). Heaven is actually an indescribable term. When we speak of the Kingdom of heaven, that is the source from which the term comes. We speak of the Kingdom of God and its presence here, just as we speak of the Son of man or Son of God. It is actually mostly a matter of semantics.

The important thing to understand is that the earth, as we now know it, with its flesh and carnality, will pass away. Likewise, the heavens and its lightning, thunder, and other elements that bring devastation to mankind will also pass away. But all things will assume the rightful places that God intended them to occupy in the first place.

God found the earth "without form, and void." In order for the earth to be "void," there must have been some forms of life existing upon it before God found it formless. Just as a check cannot be voided until it has been written, so the earth must have known life before God created mankind in the persons of Adam and Eve.

It is a fact, then, that there have been other creations upon the earth. We have evidence of that in fossils which have been unearthed. Those who think that man

QUESTIONS AND DISCUSSION 101

was the first creature upon the earth always have difficulty in accepting what geologists and archeologists tell
us about creation. The earth has been here for millions
and millions of years, and animals of one type and
another have also been here for millions and millions of
years. But man has been here for merely thousands of
years.

This is an area where the Church, in her ignorance,
has turned off much of the intelligence of the world. God
did not write or intend the Bible as a book of science.
What we need to understand is that the earth was just as
the Book of Genesis said it was - without form and void.
It was an earth without any semblance of order, and
God created Adam and Eve to bring that formless earth
back under His dominion.

If Adam and Eve had acted as they should have, their
dominion would have eventually covered the whole
earth. But they failed when they acted according to their
mind of reason, and because they failed, God had to
give us a plan of recovery and redemption in the second
Adam, Jesus Christ. Now the second Adam produced
the Church, and if the Church fulfills the commission
she has been given, she will bring Jesus Christ back to
the earth once again.

If the first Adam failed, how do we know that the
second Adam won't fail also? We know He **cannot** fail
because Jesus Christ, the second Adam, was God Incarnate, and we see in Him such victory that we know that
He can never fail. When we do things in the name of
Jesus Christ, we will not fail either. If we do things in our
own name or in our own power, we will fail many, many
times, but the power and righteousness we have in the
name of Jesus Christ can **never** fail.

Heaven and earth, as we know them now, will pass

away, but the earth itself will take on a new form. John's revelation tells us, "There will be a **new heaven** and a **new earth** ," and that will be where the righteousness of Jesus Christ dwells.

Will you please explain more about the Spirit of Balaam?

Balaam assumed that the first time Israel committed a sin, he had the right to curse Israel. He also assumed that God was so righteous and untouchable that He would not recover Israel (Jude 11). Both were horrible assumptions on his part. Another man who made a wrongful assumption about whether or not God would forgive Israel was Hosea, whom God caused to marry a harlot.

The concept we must understand is that we do not pick and choose for God; only a mature Church can do that. If God had allowed us to make all our own choices across the years, some would have had lily-white churches, while others would have had all-black churches or all-Brazilian churches or all-African churches. Despite God's biblical precepts, we have still tried to do that. We cannot drive down the street without seeing names such as "African Church" or "European Church." It should be obvious that God cannot trust us to make these types of decisions for ourselves.

We need to know that we must learn to transcend those differences and anything else that keeps us from seeing as Christ sees so that we might achieve the maturity that can bring about the totally unified Church that God is looking for.

I have never seen the word "rapture" in the Bible. Is it there? If not, why is it used?

No, the word "rapture" is not used in the Bible, but it is a term which means "to catch up" or "to be caught up." For example, suppose a girl has been waiting months for her boyfriend to come home from the Army. She has gone to the airport to meet him and when she finally sees him get off the plane, in her great excitement she cannot help but run across the runway to meet him. How would we describe her emotional state? We might say that she is raptured. Therefore, we can consider "rapture" to be a term meaning either "catching away" or "exuberance."

Rapture is a term that has been applied by certain denominations and particularly by the Pentecostal and Evangelical Churches. I myself was a proponent of that term for many years because that was all I had ever heard taught. I was raised to believe that when God was ready, the time would come when the Church would be caught up to meet Christ in the air and He would take the Church away. While they were gone, the house of Jacob, or Israel, would be tried for seven years, the time of the great tribulation. At the end of the period of tribulation, Christ would return with His saints and establish the millennial reign.

These are merely symbolic terms. A millennium is a period of a thousand years, and we teach that 1000 is a term of completion, since it is a multiple of ten. There is no higher number than ten - eleven is ten plus one; twelve is ten plus two; twenty is two tens; and so on. The millennium, therefore, symbolizes the time of the total and complete reign of Christ.

But literal teachings about the millennium held that Christ would take the Church away and hold them in a safe place while Israel was being tried. Then Christ would return to rule in Jerusalem on the throne of His father, David, bringing about a restoration of the literal tribes of national Israel. During this period, the heads of the tribes of Israel would again rule and reign with Christ for a thousand years, and at the end of that time, Satan would be loosed for a short time (the period of Gog and Magog). After that would come the Great White Throne Judgment and the new heaven and the new earth.

It is my judgment that the theory of the rapture was fine for the day in which it was taught and that God used it at that time. But that is not the message that will mature the Church today. The term itself is not used in the Bible; it is simply a facet of a theory that has been taught by certain segments of the Church throughout the years.

How do you view the development and importance of the family in the process of maturing the Bride?

I think the family is of tremendous importance because the family is the first place we learn the principle of submission and the place God wants a man to learn how to rule his own household. The Bible tells us, "For if a man know not how to rule his own house, how shall he take care of the church of God?" (I Timothy 3:5). Properly understood, I believe the family is a place of learning how to be faithful over a few things so that God can then make us faithful over the Church and finally over the Kingdom.

Problems have arisen because we have had so much

division in the family unit. A family must have a spiritual head. Many erroneous teachings have come out recently about whether a wife should submit to her husband if he is not a spiritual man. She would submit to him in natural areas, including benevolence, but she would not submit to him in spiritual areas.

The seed of the Kingdom of God rests with a spiritual man who is the head of his home and a spiritual woman who is his helpmeet and spiritual handmaiden. More and more I believe that God is looking for example families and He will not give up on a family that has made a mistake, such as a divorce. God will join people together into a family unit with a spiritual head and a spiritual handmaiden, but remember that the family was originally God's idea. The family was never Satan's idea, and that is why he so wars the family.

I maintain that the family has become somewhat of a sacred cow today. Many people attempt to use the family as the primary setting for religious exercises, but they have failed to understand the proper role of the family as it relates to the Church. Many of the greatest evils in society today are more prevalent in the family than anywhere else: incest, pornography, refrigerators full of alcohol, medicine cabinets full of drugs, more homicides than anywhere else.

The home is not sacred because it is a home. It becomes sacred only as it is obedient to Christ. It becomes sacred when the man becomes the image of Christ and the woman becomes the symbol of the Bride of Christ in that household.

The family is vital, but there must be a spiritual head and a spiritual helpmeet in order for it to function as it should. If both are not there, God has made provision for that circumstance. The Bible says, "When my father and mother put me down, when my husband or wife forsakes me, then the Church becomes my spiritual help."

What is the call of the church? Its call is to care for widows and orphans, to support the family, and sometimes to be an alternative to it. But there is no difficulty when we properly understand that the family is God's institution on the earth. The only institution, however, that God **officially** established is the Church. Some people might say, "God established the home in the Garden of Eden," but He didn't. He simply established male and female.

Jesus said, "**I will build my church;** and the gates of hell shall not prevail against it" (Matthew 16:18). We must put our priorities in order. Anyone who says, "God is first, my family is second, and the church is third, fourth, or fifth," does not know the Bible. God and the church cannot be separated, and anyone who tries to do so has the spirit of the antichrist. The proper order is: God and Church; family; self; other things, such as one's job. Don't let family-oriented authors who make millions of dollars from their books (some of whom, unfortunately, have never even known family relationships) convince you that taking your family to the lake on the Lord's Day is more important than taking them to church. **The most important thing that you can do is to obey God.** If a family has a spiritual head, he is going to want to take his family to church on the Lord's Day and is going to want them to tithe and give to the Lord.

So much prostitution of the truth is taking place today because of the word "family," and a family apart from God can be dead wrong. We must learn the proper relationship of the family to the Church as the Word of God teaches it.

When the Church is called away, will judgment from God fall upon the world? Will there be a tribulation?

In the Word of the Lord when Jesus Christ returns, He is depicted with power coming out of His mouth which has tremendous authority over the earth. I believe that when Christ returns, the Church will already have taken such dominion over the earth that it will more or less be just a matter of cleaning up.

I do believe there is a hell. I don't know **where** it is, but I know **what** it is. It is a place of confinement for evil spirits. Hell was made for the devil because he was a rebellious creature who raised himself up to challenge the dominion of God. When he rebelled against God's authority, God had to create a place of confinement for Him. If any of us should go to hell, we would go as intruders because hell was **never** created for us.

People are not sent to hell because of sex, tobacco or alcohol, for they are generally only by-products of a wrong lifestyle. People are sent to hell because of disobedience and rebellion. God has to have a hell, for there could be no heavenly existence on the earth if there were not a hell where rebellious spirits could be confined.

Will there be a tribulation? We are in tribulation right now. Tribulation describes a state of being, not a period of time. Paul said, "When we were with you, we told you before that we should suffer tribulation" (I Thessalonians 3:4), and Jesus said, "In the world ye shall have tribulation" (John 16:33). Part of the state of the Christian journey is the tribulation that accompanies it.

Some people believe this period will be followed by

the binding of Satan, but for the person who knows that he or she is a child of God, Satan has **already** been bound. But when the general Church assumes its rightful place in God and crushes the serpent's head, then will be fulfilled God's prophecy in the Garden:

> And I will put enmity between thee
> and the woman, and between thy seed
> and her seed; it shall bruise thy head,
> and thou shalt bruise his heel. (Genesis
> 3:15)

The devil is already bound. How could we take chains and bind the devil? How can a spirit be physically bound? The term has been misunderstood. It is intended to convey the concept that Satan is bound when we know who we are in God, when we know how to use the Word of God, and when we know the power that resides in the name of Jesus Christ.

Tribulation is part of the Christian walk, but it is also a relative term. It may be difficult for someone who has been imprisoned in Russia for preaching the gospel to believe that a greater tribulation still lies ahead.

Jesus said that the hour had come for Him to be glorified. Was He referring to some aspect of His death on the cross? Does becoming the glorified Church also involve death?

Definitely! As a matter of fact, looking at the life of Jesus Christ shows us that before we can be glorified, there are certain stages we must go through. The new birth cannot be separated from being baptized into

Jesus' death. That is the whole thrust of water baptism. Unfortunately, we have thought of it only as an outward evidence of an inward grace, and that is far too simplistic. It is a literal changing of kingdoms, from the kingdom of darkness to the Kingdom of light. When we are baptized, we need to have a full knowledge and understanding of what we are doing.

Jesus said, "Those who are saved and are baptized, those who are born again and baptized will be saved." If you have not been baptized, you have missed a vital, necessary opportunity, and I wouldn't give you much of a chance for what might happen to you. We enter into that new Kingdom by baptism, and we are crucified with Christ. After the crucifixion comes the resurrection when we are risen with Christ. That is not a future event; we are risen with Christ **now.** Before we can become as the risen, mature Christ or the mature Body of Christ, we next ascend with Jesus, and the Bible tells us that we are lifted to sit in heavenly places with Him. Following our ascension, we are then glorified with Christ.

We have the same progression in the process of the Church's maturity that Christ had in His own ministry. We have death, resurrection, ascension, maturity, and glorification. Even as we, as the Church, are crucified, we are also tried and tested, and through much tribulation and sorrow, we finally arrive at the place of ruling and reigning with Christ where we stand in His authority and sit, as it were, at God's right hand. Then follows the glorified Church. Whatever happened to Christ must also happen to the Church.

How do we, individually and as a Church, form a relationship with the Lord God, and what steps do we follow?

If a man say, I love God, and hateth
his brother, he is a liar: for he that loveth
not his brother whom he hath seen,
how can he love God whom he hath not
seen? And this commandment have we
from him, That he who loveth God love
his brother also. (I John 4:20-21)

This passage of scripture tells us why Jesus said, "You must start with the members of my Body." People who say, "I'm going to get saved and spend my Sundays on my boat," don't understand that they cannot do that. We cannot deny the existence of Christ's Body here on earth and still say, "I accept His existence in heaven."

We begin developing our relationship with God by hearing the Word of truth, by joining ourselves to a Body of believers, and then by growing in the grace and knowledge of the Lord Jesus Christ. There is no room for separatist or independent attitudes. We are all part of the Body of Christ, submitted one to the other and interacting in such a way that we recognize our brothers and sisters.

Where do you begin such a relationship? Begin it with the family of God. Become involved. Once you accept Jesus Christ and are baptized, you come out of the kingdom of darkness into the Kingdom of light. By an act of your will, you declare, "I deny the kingdom of darkness and I accept the Kingdom of light." You must make a commitment and move toward keeping and honoring it. As you grow in fellowship, you also grow in the knowledge of the Lord Jesus Christ, and as you continue to grow, God will begin to trust you with more and more spiritual power and authority.

Where and how do you develop fellowship with God? You develop fellowship with Him by developing fellowship within His Church. You cannot love God unless you love your brothers and sisters in Christ, and you cannot trust God until you learn to trust others. You cannot submit to God until you learn submission to those who are over you in the Lord. These are principles of the Kingdom.

Is it possible that the second coming of Christ will be manifested as the glorious, healed Body of Christ rather than in the form of Jesus returning in his physical body?

That doctrine has been preached, but I believe that there must be a Bride and a groom. I believe also that the Church is always described as the Bride and Jesus Christ as the bridegroom.

Jesus Christ will always be a personality. He will always be the glorified Christ, and He will always be the manifestation of God in the flesh. I believe that as the glorified Church, we will have personal interaction with Jesus Christ as King of kings and Lord of lords.

I believe, too, that Jesus Christ will return in the same manner in which He went away, and we have scriptural proof of this.

> *Ye men of Galilee, why stand ye gazing up into heaven? this same Jesus, which is taken up from you into heaven, shall so come in like manner as ye have seen him go into heaven. (Acts 1:11)*

Jesus ascended as the glorified Christ, and He will
return as the glorified Christ.

Because Jesus promised that He would always be
with us, I would consider the idea of eternity incomplete
without **knowing** that Jesus Christ would personally
rule and reign. In his revelation, John wrote,

> *And I saw no temple therein: for the
> Lord God Almighty and the Lamb are
> the temple of it. And the city had no
> need of the sun, neither of the moon, to
> shine in it: for the glory of God did
> lighten it, and the Lamb is the light
> thereof. (Revelation 21:22-23)*

> *And there shall be no night there;
> and they need no candle, neither light
> of the sun; for the Lord God giveth
> them light: and they shall reign for ever
> and ever. (Revelation 22:5)*

That means that the real and actual presence of the
glorified Christ will rule in the New Jerusalem forever
and ever.

**Can the separation that takes place at the table of
the Lord be a separation of truth and untruth within
ourselves on an individual rather than on a collective
basis?**

Yes. The table of the Lord is at work constantly.
When we come to the table of the Lord, the separation

sometimes takes place between the carnal and the spiritual or between men's opinions and what God says. But sometimes there must be a separation such as Judas experienced. Hopefully, though, there will always be that internal separation that surfaces the goodness of God in us. That is what I pray for every time we come to the table of the Lord.

What do you mean by the term "transcending work of the Holy Spirit"?

I do not believe that we can direct the Holy Spirit. The scriptures tell us that "...one and the selfsame Spirit" divides "to every man severally **as he will**" (I Corinthians 12:11). Sometimes we want to tell the Holy Spirit whom to call to a certain mission, where to build, or what to do. We must learn to become so sensitive in discernment that we know when it is the Holy Spirit and when it is man's opinion at work. The Holy Spirit transcends every other thing that we would do. If I made a statement and the Holy Spirit transcended it, I might later say, "The Holy Spirit has transcended the statement that I made. While it may have been a good statement, the best thing is always what God says."

Always leave room for the Holy Spirit to work because He is the Spirit of truth. "When he, the Spirit of truth, is come, he will guide you into all truth" (John 16:13). The Spirit transcends any human decision or appointment. When I ask someone the question, "Has God spoken to you?", that transcends anything else I could say. Knowing what God has said transcends us or anything we could ever say or do.

What is going to be changed about the generation that will not die?

Every limitation will be removed. The corrupt body must take on incorruption. For example, now we can hear and see at limited distances, and we can carry our physical bodies only so far. The Bible tells us that Jesus would be in one place and then suddenly He would be gone and be somewhere else. That excites me because I don't care much for flying anyway! That may sound a little foolish, but is it really? We are limited now by natural laws. Our communication is limited to the written word or to word-of-mouth. Every once in awhile, we have such a close relationship with another person that we can communicate without saying a word. We communicate with our eyes or with other deeper means of expression. I believe the time will come when all these aspects that we now know will be lifted to a much greater and higher dimension.

When we can be trusted because we have proven ourselves trustworthy, all the limitations will be gone, and we will be known even as we are known (I Corinthians 13:12). We will know one another as God knows us, because nothing will be hidden.

Is the Kingdom of God going to be established no matter what, or is it an alternative? Could it be that the plan of God will not work and the result will be similar to the days of Noah?

Jesus said that even the gates of hell would not prevail against His Kingdom. That promise was never made to

Adam and Eve. Nothing was ever said about the gates of hell not prevailing against them. But that promise was explicitly given to the Church, and because that is the key to establishing the Kingdom, I believe that at some time and in some generation, we will hold onto these promises to such degree that the Kingdom will no longer be a matter of an option or an alternative; it will be an absolute act of a sovereign God. All God is waiting for now is **us.**

I do say, however - although it frightens me to do so - that I believe we could come so close to establishing the Kingdom, yet fail in our commission and cause some other generation to have to fulfill our responsibility.

If all the circumstances had been in place, I believe the Kingdom could have been established a thousand years ago. But things then had not been fulfilled as they have been now. All God is waiting for now is **us.**

Our goal must be to effect the healing of the wounded Body of Christ and in so doing, bring about the unity that will allow the Spirit and the Bride to declare that all things are now ready and in order and that the Bride is mature and prepared. Then in a strong, clear voice that the world is waiting to hear, the Spirit and the Bride can say together, "Come, Lord Jesus. Come."